The Marriage Relationship

A Model for Intervention and Care

Douglas A. Lawton

LIVITY BOOKS

THE MARRIAGE RELATIONSHIP:
A MODEL FOR INTERVENTION AND CARE

ISBN 978-1-941632-15-4

Copyright © 2009 by Douglas A. Lawton

All rights reserved. No portion of this book may be reproduced in any form or by any means, electronic or mechanical, including photocopying and recording, or by any information storage or retrieval system without the written permission of the owner of this copyright or the publisher.

Published by
Livity Books
West Palm Beach, Florida 33416

Table of Contents

	Preface	7
	Introduction	9
1	Essential Building Blocks of Marriage	11
2	Contrary Views on Marital Dysfunction	17
3	Commonly-held Interpretations of Scripture	39
4	Psycho-social Related Issues	57
5	Consequences of Separation	69
6	Coping with Separation	89
7	Coping with Relationship Baggage	105
8	Care for a Troubled Relationship	111
9	Conclusion of the Whole Matter	149
	Bibliography	157

Preface

Most of what has been written in Scripture concerning the institution of marriage has been written in response to human experience or in anticipation of the predictable. Albeit, the biblical writers did not anticipate nor concern themselves with every conceivable societal or personal issue which might have arisen; general principles informed specific situations. Accordingly, the biblical writers did not pretend to offer wide-scale prescriptions to every problem impacting marriage.

Doctrine evolved out of human experience. In other words, biblical doctrine was not created in a vacuum but was impacted by the existential reality of human experience. Without changing divine absolutes, using divine principles the biblical writers responded to the context of the individual or community, and as such modified or elaborated on certain doctrines so as to give more currency to the relevant doctrine, the spirit of the law often prevailing over the letter of the law. Case in point, Jesus and Paul in their treatment of divorce and remarriage.

As far as divine institutions are concerned, God's ideal is affected by the existential reality of human experience including the inescapable reality of sin. This does not mean, however, that God has changed His mind concerning the original intent, design or desire for these institutions. On the contrary, but we should take cognizance that human experience, particularly as it is affected by sin, has significantly affected the nature and viability of institutions of which people are a part.

Certain institutions were created on the premise that they would fulfill the will of God for the development of the human family and the maintenance of social order in the world. It is apparent that where this is not happening the will of God is being undermined. History has shown that institutions such as marriage (the family), the church (religion) and government, for example, instead of promoting good may be corrupted and may be used as a cover for evil. They may be oppressive and inimical to the best interest of the people they were designed to help and protect. How to correct this anomaly has been a source of controversy and frustration for both the religious and non-religious.

Unfortunately, while there has been readiness to identify with the struggles of people affected by good institutions gone bad and willingness to support the parties involved in practical ways, people in a troubled marriage are regarded less sympathetically, especially in religious communities. This presents a serious challenge for a spouse who does not have the support in place to make sense of his/her experience and who wants to do the will of God but feels trapped in a dysfunctional marriage. The unexamined tradition of the Church and an unsympathetic public – people who view every divorce as sinful and divorcees as lepers to be avoided – add to the dilemma.

This book is about helping people to take a more realistic and biblical view of marriage, while at the same time encouraging them to fulfill God's ideal for the marriage relationship. I hope you will enjoy the journey.

Introduction

God's Response to Aloneness

Marriage is as old as the entrance of humankind on the planet. Marriage was instituted by God in response to the aloneness of the first human-being, Adam. Since it was not good that man should be alone, God provided a woman to journey through life as a married partner with the man whom He created (Genesis 2:18-25). Accordingly, from the inception of marriage it has been commonly understood that wife means woman or female, and that husband means man or male.

From time immemorial, marriage has been recognized to be the most basic institution of society and fundamental to the development of the human family. Marriage is fundamental to the development f the human family insofar as it affirms male-female sexual identity, provides the proper context for the propagation of the human race, augurs for the socio-psychological, physical, moral and spiritual development of the human specie.

Because marriage is linked to the family and the home, marriage is regarded as a significant and sacred milestone. As such, people in every culture aspire toward marriage and the establishment of their own nuclear family. Clarke averred that marriage is widely sought after, because it brings with it a certain air of respectability and class (Clarke, 1974).

Indeed, marriage is widely sought after for various reasons, and is God's answer to man's aloneness. But the reality is many married couples still feel alone, or have experienced an emotional disconnect, although sharing the same physical space for many years. It could be that some couples might have entered marriage for the wrong reasons. Marrying for the wrong reason/s, misperceptions, inappropriate behavior, all of the above or a combination of unwholesome factors may negatively impact the marriage relationship. Some couples may live in a dysfunctional marriage for years. Others may try to fix it. Still, some end it in divorce.

Although offering insights on what constitutes a healthy marriage, the text objectively examines causes of marital dysfunction and divorce, and guides the reader toward success in remarriage. The book is written from a Christian perspective and reflects that bias.

An important feature of the text is that it helps the reader navigate the reality of marital dysfunction or divorce and the desire for a new beginning. Unlike most books on the marriage relationship, this text focuses on neglected areas of the relationship spectrum, divorce and remarriage. As such, the book carefully scouts these paradigms and attempts to help the reader reconciled to the reality of divorce and the prospect of remarriage via pastoral care.

The word 'pastoral' has its origin in the Bible. It means shepherding – a quality of care that includes God in the picture. According to Stone and Duke, *All Christians need to operate with a theological template. Without it spiritual assessment of what is happening with a troubled parishioner, or in one's Christian life, will surely result in an inadequate theological response* (1996, p. 42). As such, it is imperative that an understanding of the elements constituting a viable Christian marriage be apprehended.

1
Essential Building Blocks of Marriage

Throughout history, marriage has been widely accepted and supported, though formalized differently in various cultures. The only area of dispute has been the number of wives a man may have, legally. That is, whether a man may have only one wife during his lifetime, one wife at a time, or more than one wife at the same time. Both monogamy and polygamy, however, have been practiced by different cultures from ancient civilization to the present time.

Although there have been and continues to be differences as to how the union is conceived and how marriage is practiced, marriage continues to have a pride of place in every culture. People in the West have been influenced a great deal by the Judeo-Christian ethic hence views on marriage largely reflect that of Christianity, and more specifically on interpretations of the Bible.

There are several building blocks essential to the institution of marriage. These building blocks are important, because they are not only integral to the institution of marriage but are the very foundation on which a viable marriage is built. The features comprising a viable marriage are:

- Constitutionality and sociality
- Congenitality
- Conjugality
- Consensuality
- Commitability
- Spirituality

Needless to say, if one or more of these foundation stones are compromised or is no longer present in the relationship, the marriage may collapse or become irretrievably broken down.

The constitutionality and sociality of marriage
Although marriage is a private affair, it is also a public concern; it is a social contract. As such, marriage includes a legal representative and witnesses to the fact. That is, for the marriage to be legally binding, those who pledge themselves in marriage must necessarily do so before a duly constituted or legal authority and in the presence of witnesses. In other words, the person presiding over the marriage ceremony must be a qualified marriage officer; certain legal conditions must be met, and the marriage must take place in the presence of witnesses, for the marriage to be recognized as being legally constituted.

The congenitality of marriage
Marriage speaks to a common or communal relationship. It is God's answer to a person's aloneness. When God made Adam, every creature on earth had another after its kind except Adam. It was necessary therefore for God to create another like Adam to support and accompany him along the journey of human existence. The relationship, of necessity had to be congenial. But as a married couple, it was also necessary that Adam's companion be of a different gender. An appreciation for gender differences, the unique physiological and psychological differences that the partners bring to the relationship would go a far way in enhancing the quality of human development. So in keeping with God's desire for marriage, God created a woman. The essence of marriage therefore is con-

genital companionship. Marriage involves a male-female relationship.

The conjugality of marriage
Marriage does not only involve companionship or a social relationship between a man and a woman, but it also involves sex. Marriage is not just social; it is physical. It is sex between a man and his wife that consummates the union. And, within reason, sex continues to play an integral part in bonding the couple and in enhancing their marriage. Marriage is therefore an intimate and emotional affair. It is a one-flesh relationship – the couple expresses love for each other by relating socially and sexually.

By their physical presence and physical contact the couple creates a social and emotional bond, which gives them the exclusive right over the body of each other, and the responsibility to care for one another. As married partners, they share in the continued pleasure of a social and sexual relationship – in the fulfillment of the purposes of God in expanding the human race by producing after their kind, and in their occupation and stewardship over planet earth. A marriage exists where the couple is connected physically, socially, sexually and emotionally.

The consent of marriage
But that is not all. The man has a choice in the matter; so does the woman. And together they must agree to become husband and wife. Marriage is a covenant relationship. A covenant is by two and is necessarily consensual. There must be the willingness to leave all others and to cleave to one's wife/husband. Consenting to the marriage continues to be integral to the maintenance of the relationship.

The commitment of marriage
Accordingly, a Christian marriage involves mutual commitment. This presupposes genuine love for each other as the commitment is to one man and to one woman until death. According to Peck (1978, p. 140):

> *Whether it be shallow or not, commitment is the foundation, the bedrock of any genuinely loving relationship. Deep commitment does not guarantee the success of the relationship but does help more than any other factor to assure it... [I]t is our sense of commitment after the wedding which makes possible the transition from falling in love to genuine love.*

So the ethos of marriage is two persons covenanting under God to commit to each other until the death of either partner. As the unseen but Supreme Witness, God recognizes their vows and expects the couple to honour them. As such, a Christian marriage is a sacred covenant. It includes God into the picture.

The spirituality of marriage
God is the third party in marriages. He is the One who decreed marriage, and is the Supreme Witness to the fact. Marriage was not intended for a select group of people; God ordained marriage for humanity on the whole. *It is not good that man should be alone* (Genesis 2:18) is a reference to the human race, or wherever people may be found. The mandate to marry speaks to God's concern for all His creatures – to satisfy people's need for companionship – the need for social order – and the need for the propagation and development of the human race. Marriage is therefore a fusion of the spirit as well as the body. However, it is the fusion of the spirit that gives currency to the fusion of the body. Hence, if a person's spirit is not endeared to the body with which it fuses, there is really no bonding of the couple at all; the absence of which raises serious questions regarding the validity and sustainability of the marriage. The couple must not only become one flesh, but also one spirit. In fact, a man must be joined unto his wife in spirit in order to validate the one flesh relationship (Eph. 5:25-33).

Therefore, integral to marital counseling is an appreciation for the essential features which make up a marriage, otherwise expressed as the foundation stones of constitutionality, congenitality, conjugality, consensuality, commitability and spirituality. But success in marriage doesn't just happen because It has these elements. A marriage is far more complicated than that. There are other features which are integral to the success of the relationship. In general, problems develop in marriages when couples begin to take each other or the marriage for granted and by failing to secure the essential elements of marriage and to expand its features.

Being married is not the ultimate goal; staying married is an enormous challenge, which takes a lot of work and a lifetime of commitment. Albeit a major milestone in one's life, marriage is important but it is the relationship that counts. To stay married, a couple needs to be constantly working at the relationship. Initially it involves learning to adjust to each other, the accepting of individual differences and diverse points-of-view. Moreover, the couple needs to be growing together intellectually, emotionally and spiritually for their marriage to succeed. Too wide a gap between spouses in any of these areas may be a source of discord between them, and may bring about a strain on the relationship.

In addition, since the couple generally comes from different backgrounds and each person is his/her 'own self,' married partners will need to learn to adjust to each other without violating each other's personhood or boundaries. Violation of boundaries and attempts at manipulating each other into thinking or acting in the same way may derail the marriage.

Couples therefore need to learn the language of love – in order to communicate needs and desires – in order to communicate appreciation or satisfaction – and in order to communicate hurts or disappointments respectfully. Honest and respectful communication will go a far way in building the relationship. On the other hand, denial, suppression of the truth and unloving or destructive confrontations are likely to destroy it.

A successful marriage will not happen just because the couple said "I do." It takes conscious effort, self-disclosure, self-development, knowledge and patience to build a harmonious relationship. Difficulties as a result of personal weaknesses or the unavoidable circumstances of life may pose a tremendous challenge at times for the newly and not so newly-wed, but these are necessary aids (not ills) to help couples grow and to bring them in the know. Experience builds character, and if carefully evaluated teaches wisdom.

Unfortunately, many couples succumb to life's challenges, partly due to ignorance, immaturity, and, among others, belief in all kinds of myths. The experiences of life can help them to understand things differently. The pastoral counselor is strategically located to help dispel some of these myths, to provide valuable service to those seeking help with a troubled marriage and to persons going through a divorce.

2

Contrary Views on Marital Dysfunction

In Christendom, marriage is viewed as a sacred cow. Anything therefore that threatens or shakes this institution is viewed unfavorably or evokes serious concern. Interestingly, the divorce rate among the Christian community is similar to the divorce rate among non-Christians. In light of the spiraling divorce rate and its negative impact on society's social fabric, concern for the family is being expressed worldwide by Christians and non-Christians alike. And since divorce seemingly threatens the wholeness of the social fabric of society, the tendency is to view every divorce in an unfavorable light. This is true especially among members of the Christian community.

Ironically, divorcees belonging to the Christian community apparently suffer most; and unnecessarily so because of attitudes in the Church toward divorce and remarriage. In many churches divorcees are regarded as spiritual lepers to be discarded or persons to be ostracized. As a result, divorcees' wounds often go untended and the pain of divorce is unnecessarily prolonged. This is partly so because some pastors wrongly presume that the *unequal yoke* relates to religion only; and so, once the couple professes Christianity they are encouraged, pressured even, to get married without being given a chance to really get to know each other well enough to make an informed decision.

It is believed that since the couple is right for each other by virtue of their "common faith," they should be able to work out whatever difficulty they might experience as married partners. As a result, divorce in most churches of the Caribbean is a big taboo. In many Christian churches, enduring a dysfunctional marriage (irrespective of the nature of the dysfunction) is viewed as a sign of Christian piety. That being the case, many church leaders are insensitive toward parishioners who see divorce as an option in dealing with a troubled marriage; those who are bold enough to obtain a divorce are punished. They are treated as second-class Christians and are no longer able to hold certain positions in their churches.

Like their parishioners, Church leaders are neither immune to divorce and remarriage nor from the repercussions of these realities. The impact sometimes is even greater. As for some, their careers are on the line. Coupled with the pain of divorce itself, the spiritual and emotional burden of admitting personal failure to their flock and the unsympathetic attitude of Church and society toward them, many divorcee-pastors have found themselves *caught between a rock and a hard place.*

To add to divorcees' dilemma, there is confusion among the Church community regarding the issues of divorce and remarriage, as the views are varied and often contradictory. Some churches will not allow divorce on any ground whatsoever; some will allow divorce but not remarriage; and some will allow divorce and remarriage albeit for different reasons.

Many churches in the Caribbean are connected to parent bodies or affiliates in North America and Europe. As such, perceptions of local churches regarding "spiritual" matters are usually informed by their denominational organizations. There are, however, local bodies which have held on to beliefs handed down by the parent organization long after these beliefs have been modified or changed. Adding to the confusion is the fact that issues of divorce and remarriage are seldom discussed publicly.

The fact that the issues of divorce and remarriage are given scant attention in most churches highlights the importance of this text. This chapter presents findings of qualitative research conducted in Jamaica by the writer between 2003 and 2004. As part of the research, two questionnaires were developed, *The Divorce Questionnaire* and *Church Leaders' Divorce Questionnaire*. The questionnaires were designed so that respondents could freely report on their perceptions of divorce and remarriage, and the effects of divorce on divorcees and on divorcee-children. The sample of respondents included sixty-nine persons belonging to the church community.

The first questionnaire, *The Divorce Questionnaire*, was administered in 2003. Because of the sensitive nature of the study, and the difficulty in getting people to talk about their issues, this researcher took persons who were readily available and willing to participate in the survey. The sample is therefore a convenience sample. It must be pointed out as well that the survey was largely conducted among urban middle-class professionals, age ranging from 31-50.

The second questionnaire, *Church Leaders' Divorce Questionnaire*, was administered in 2004. Thirteen religious leaders from various religious organizations completed the questionnaire. An additional seven church leaders were interviewed to include the perspectives of their denominations in the survey, thereby expanding the list to twenty. Like the first survey, the sample was a convenience sample, obtained through referrals of friends and associates.

The findings, however, cannot be used to make generalizations, bearing in mind that most of the sample came from urban middle class professionals in the case of *The Divorce Questionnaire*. In the case of the *Church Leaders' Divorce Questionnaire*, it must be borne in mind that within some religious organizations, there are various views on divorce and remarriage, and that the official ruling of the denomination is not complied with by all member churches, in some instances.

Notwithstanding, the research provides additional insight into divorce and remarriage from a local perspective. The information gleamed corroborates earlier research and contextualizes the findings *vis-à- vis* the general readings.

A series of questions were asked to ascertain the level of support divorcees received before and after the divorce, among other things. Forty-eight percent (33) of the 69 respondents sought counseling before the divorce, and of those who sought counseling 50% thought it was beneficial; 39% sought counseling after the divorce, while 67% of that number thought it was beneficial. Only 8% of divorcees were part of a support group. This underscores the point of divorcees' neglect by the Church and the wider society.

That counseling does not necessarily prevent divorce is evident; according to the data couples in a troubled marriage stand a 50:50 chance of benefiting from counseling. However, the success of counseling is relative to the time the counseling commenced, the individual's openness to the process, and in part to the skill of the counselor. Rice (2001) believes that the earlier a couple in a troubled marriage seeks counseling, the more likely it will succeed.

For counseling to effect any meaningful change, both spouses have to be open to the process; they have to be willing to work through their problems. At times couples are no longer interested in the relationship and sometimes one party has an interest and the other does not. This retards the process. In addition, couples sometimes seek counseling because they were sent by the court hence they are not as committed to the process as those who initiate counseling themselves. Other times, they need help to end the relationship amicably or to minimize the trauma of an imminent divorce.

Respondents to the survey were asked to state the main reason/s for the divorce. Several reasons were given. The most common was incompatibility (23 people or 33.3%). Communication and infidelity tied for second place. Sixteen persons or 23.2% identified communication as being the second most common cause for the divorce. Infidelity also ranked second by virtue of the same percentage. Financial problems ranked third: fourteen or 20.3% of the persons polled identified financial distress as causing the break-down of the marriage.

The fact that incompatibility ranked as the number one problem leading to divorce underscores the need for premarital counseling. There are several possible reasons for incompatibility in relationships:

- Couples might have got married for the wrong reason
- Couples might not have taken the time to really know each other.
- Couples might have failed to discuss relevant issues and potential causes of conflict.
- Couples might have been of the mistaken notion that they could change their partner.
- The relationship might have been based more on biology than psychology.
- There might have been unrealistic expectations.
- One party might have outgrown the other in an area critical to personal and corporate development.

Communication and infidelity, having ranked second, are understandable. Improper communication or inadequate communication can easily undermine a marriage. Wholesome communication is integral to the bonding of the couple. According to Rice (2001), surveys in America showed poor communication as having the most damaging effect on a marriage. Married couples, generally, do not communicate as well as they should, or as much as they should. Plus, problem-solving skills, a vital part of the communication process, is sometimes lacking. This is due in part to the fact that the average Jamaican male is not as verbally expressive as he should be and is unskilled in communicating feelings intelligently. As a youth, he was socialized to solve problems with his fists or learned to just walk away. He was also socialized to believe that he is a 'sissy' if he is a talkative person and if he expresses 'softness,' such as crying when hurt or in pain.

The Jamaican male, however, prides himself on his sexual prowess, so infidelity is a 'common assault.' *By conquering several women sexually and siring numerous offspring, one of patriarchy's original symbols of power is extravagantly displayed, even if the women and children are not protected or provided for* (Miller, 1991, p. 267). His penis power gives him a sense of identity. It appears women are not as promiscuous, although unafraid to flaunting their sexuality.

Given the high cost of living in Jamaica and the general state of the economy, financial problems, understandably, have a destabilizing effect on families. Many families do not cope well with financial stress. Financial stress may give rise to insecurities, feelings of resentment, anger, physical and verbal or emotional abuse, thereby undermining the relationship. The family may break apart as one partner may seek greener pastures overseas never to return. For falling on hard times, some women may abandon their husbands, treat them with disrespect, or marginalize their spouse.

Men who can no longer meet the needs of their family may become depressed, as manhood is equated with a man's role as provider. Some men may take to drinking, become withdrawn, commit suicide, or run away. The thought of being unable to provide for their families is disconcerting, to say the least. Miller (1991) made the point that marginalized men who are failing to live up to their obligations under patriarchy and who fail to live up to their own expectations, may choose any of the above, including violence as a means of escape or as a way of coping with marginalization. It is apparent that the traditional concept of the breadwinner male has affected male-female relationships, greatly impacting a man's self-image, the female's perception of him and the 'success' of some marriages.

Since money is linked to self-respect, authority and power, some men have difficulty relating to spouses who make more money than they do, while some women have difficulty respecting men who are earning less than they are making. If the man is not the main breadwinner, he is perceived to be 'a loser.' He views himself as such, and his perception is confirmed by a society that affirms his pathology. This devalued self subsequently acts out in ways that make the marriage all the more challenging, if not impossible to maintain.

Unfortunately, while essential and more so in our consumer-driven and competitive environment, an unbalanced approach to money has robbed many of the happiness they desire in their relationships. Perceptions on money and the male breadwinner paradigm as an inviolable family construct have been major sources of incongruities and the consequent disaffection in marital relationships.

In fact, it impacts our perception of sexuality in particular and role play in general. As a standard for all families, it limits creativity; it may stymie the development of a female spouse who wishes to expand her repertoire of experience to include areas traditionally dominated by the opposite sex; and may actually retard the development of men who may wish to take on certain "female" roles, especially the development of the nurturing side of their persona, without being regarded as sissies. The male breadwinner paradigm may also be responsible for the restriction of the growth of the family in general.

On the other hand, however, it may not be the male breadwinner paradigm that is at fault here, but our perception of what that means. What is certain, though, is that we need a more enlightened and reality-centered approach to marriage. Mary Faller echoed similar sentiments in her review of the book *Breadwinner Wives and the Men They Marry: How to Have a Successful Marriage While Outearning Your Husband* ("The Sunday Gleaner," March 24, 2002, pp. 8h, 9h). Faller stated that the writer of the book expressed the view that the perception that men should always be the breadwinners was insulting to both men and women. According to Faller, the author of the book has found that in the happiest couples, there are certain shared qualities in husbands, and that there are certain shared qualities in wives as well:

Shared qualities of husbands
1. Are motivated by quality of life, not money or power
2. Are non-competitive
3. Are more engaged in the lives of their families
4. Are accustomed to seeing women as leaders

Shared qualities of wives
1. Were raised to be independent
2. Have a history of being unconventional
3. Are not obsessed with career or financial success
4. Have a strong sense of themselves and the direction they have chosen

In our post-modern world, couples of most cultures are engaged in providing bread, hence should not be restricted to stereotypical roles; instead, couples should negotiate and renegotiate as the need arises, so the family on the whole may be the winner. There is therefore need to displace gender biases with notions of equality and equity. Unfortunately, many spouses are interested in equality but not equity.

Notwithstanding, the biblical model of a noble wife does not reflect gender bias at all. Instead, it presents a wife of noble character as one who is truly liberated (Prov. 31:10-31). Regrettable for some, finding the noble wife or husband remains an elusive dream. And for those already married, divorce is an ever-present reality.

The research also revealed fifty-nine percent of respondents' marriages as having ended amicably. This finding is rather surprising, and may suggests that the perception that marriages normally end in 'bad blood' is an exaggeration, or bears no resemblance to reality. The majority of marriages, having ended amicably, should have a positive effect on divorcees' relationships after the divorce, although this is not necessarily the case.

It is after the divorce that the sting of divorce is mostly felt thus requiring increased support and counseling for the couple and their children. As divorcees grieve and the reality of separation hits home, all kinds of destabilizing emotions may be unleashed. These often lead to irrational behaviours, thereby affecting the divorcees' children and the ex-spouse. Spouses may become vindictive in withholding financial support or visitation rights. Children may become depressed and act out their emotions inappropriately, and so on (Rice, 2001).

Nineteen percent of the respondents stated that their standard of living had declined, 36% reported no change, and 45% believed that their situation improved. Interestingly, 87% reported that their ex-spouse discontinued maintaining them and their children. According to Oates (1997), most families would have suffered financial distress. One explanation of the disparity between expectations and the reality of the research findings could be that husbands' contributions to homes prior to the divorce were minimal. Other explanations may include the fact that the literature spoke to mothers being housewives prior to divorce and not to a situation where both parents were employed and making significant financial contributions to the family. (In Jamaica it is customary for both partners to have a job outside the home, and it is not unusual for upper-middle class women to out-earn their men). In these cases the loss would not be as great financially. Improvement in standard of living could also be due to job promotions, bequests, improved budgeting and the practice of thrift. The findings are not too far-fetched since the research was largely conducted among urban middle class professionals. The impact would be different with the urban poor. Divorce would have a greater negative impact, as the urban poor are more interdependent, hence, more vulnerable to the loss of the bread-winner male.

Nevertheless, it has been proven, generally, that two can live cheaper than one. Fifty-eight percent of respondents reported that there were divorces in their family; 28% regretted the divorce; 39% would marry again, 9% would not and 52% were undecided. Sixty-five percent reported that divorce has changed their perception of men/women; and 44% reported having negative feelings of self.

The overwhelming number (58%) of respondents who reported divorces in their families supported the view of Bevcar and Bevcar (2003) of the ecological link between persons and their ancestors: Events of past generations have a way of repeating themselves in the present. More specifically, if one's parents were divorced, it is quite likely that their children may experience divorce themselves. Positive and negative feelings after the divorce are relative to the time when the respondents answered the questionnaire. The time gap between divorce and divorcees' response to the questionnaire ranged from 5 to 30 years. This writer believes that the time lapse between the divorce and the questionnaire would have facilitated healing, especially where divorcees were getting counseling or were a part of a support group.

It must be stated here that most of the respondents were women, the reason being women are not as averse to talking about their problems as men are. When asked if they would marry again 52% of respondents were undecided. Generally, women do not accommodate another relationship as readily as men. Divorce is a very traumatic experience. So although a significant amount of time elapsed since the divorce, understandably, some women would be extremely cautious in starting a new relationship, especially where children are involved.

Tables 1 and 2 show the results of the second survey. The survey sought to discern the effects of divorce and remarriage on leadership in the Church.

*   Not all churches polled are included in the tables.

TABLE 1 CHURCHES' VIEWS ON DIVORCE

Christian Denominations	Positions					Effect		
	Not Allowed	Allowed for Adultery	Allowed for Desertion	Allowed for Irre. Breakdown	None	Some	Major
NT Church of God	X						X
Open Bible		X					X
United Church				X	X		
Adventist		X	X		X		
Anglican				X	X		
Gospel Assembly		X	X				X
Independent Baptists		X	X				X
Union Baptist				X	X		
Methodist				X	X		
Missionary Churches		X			X		
Moravian				X	X		
United Pentecostal		X			X		
Apostolic		X					X
Nazarene				X	X		
Salvation Army				X		X	
Brethren		X	X				X
African Methodist				X	X		

1. On what grounds, if any, does your church allow divorce?

Of the 20 persons/institutions surveyed, 5% (1) reported that divorce was not allowed; 25% (5) reported that it was allowed for adultery only; and 45% (9) reported that it was allowed for the irretrievable break-down of the marriage, meaning that one or both parties are unwilling to resolve the problem/s.

2. What effect, if any, does divorce have on persons aspiring to leadership or on persons already in a leadership position in your church?

Fifty-five percent (11) reported that it had no effect; 10% (2) that it had some effect; and 35% (7) reported that it had a major effect.

TABLE 2 — CHURCHES' VIEWS ON REMARRIAGE

CONTRARY VIEWS ON MARITAL DYSFUNCTION

Christian Denominations	Positions			Effect		
	Not Allowed	Allowed for Innocent Party	Allowed for Both Guilty & Innocent	None	Some	Major
NT Church of God	X					X
Open Bible		X				X
United Church		X	X	X		
Adventist		X				
Anglican			X	X		
Gospel Assembly	X					X
Independent Baptists	X					X
Union Baptist		X				X
Methodist				X		
Missionary Churches	X					X
Moravian	X					X
United Pentecostal	X					X
Apostolic	X					X
Nazarene			X	X		
Salvation Army					X	
Brethren		X				X
African Methodist			X	X		

1. On what grounds, if any, does your church allow remarriage?

Of the 20 persons/institutions who responded to the survey, 35% (7) stated that remarriage was not allowed; 25% (5) stated it was allowed for the innocent only; and 40% (8) stated it was allowed for both parties.

2. What effect, if any, does remarriage has on persons aspiring to leadership or on persons already in a leadership position in your church?

Thirty-five percent (7) stated that it had no effect; 5% (1) stated it had some effect; and 60% (12) stated that it had a major effect.

Information Gleaned from Unstructured Interview
The unstructured interview, which followed the *Church Leaders' Questionnaire,* yielded the perspectives of various religious organizations on divorce and remarriage, including the effect of these issues on leadership in some churches. The summary below gives a fair idea as to the lack of agreement among the churches, the controversial nature of the issues, and an idea in regard to attitudes shaped by denominational positions.

Views on divorce
- Some religious organizations do not allow divorce.
- Some allow divorce for adultery only or any form of sexual sin (*pornea*).
- Some allow divorce for adultery and desertion by a non-Christian spouse.
- Desertion by a Christian spouse of another Christian in a marriage is not deemed a ground for divorce by some churches.
- Some churches allow divorce on the basis of the irretrievable break-down of the marriage.
- Some churches do not have a set position but deals with divorce on a case-by-case basis.

Views on remarriage
- Some churches will allow divorce but not remarriage.
- Some churches will allow remarriage for the "innocent" party only.
- Some churches will allow remarriage without consideration of who is to blame for the divorce.
- Some churches will not allow remarriage until they are convinced that issues from the past have been dealt with sufficiently by persons seeking remarriage.
- If at fault for the divorce, some churches will only allow the "guilty party" to remarry if the ex-spouse died or has remarried.

Effects of Divorce & Remarriage on Leadership
- If innocent, some pastors may continue to pastor after the divorce but are not allowed to remarry.
- Some pastors may be allowed to remarry and continue serving the church in the capacity of pastor only if he/she was the innocent party.
- In some churches, although the divorcee-pastor might have conformed to the reason/s allowed for divorce by the organization, the divorcee-pastor may no longer head a congregation, although that person may minister in other ways, such as being a deacon or teacher.
- Despite the reason for the divorce, some leaders will have to step down from office until the head of the denomination is convinced that healing has taken place before divorcees are allowed to function again as head of a congregation.
- If the divorce was not obtained for reasons allowed by the denomination, divorcees may not be allowed to hold any office in the church.
- If at fault, the divorcee-pastor may head a congregation as long as he/she remains unmarried.
- Some churches do not consistently abide by the 'official' policy of their denomination.
- Individual churches may not share the 'official' position of the denomination and hence some pastors make judg-

ments as they deem fit.
- There is a stigma attached to divorcees in most churches, though in varying degrees.
- There is no formal support group for divorcees in the churches surveyed. The pastor may provide some level of counseling prior to the divorce but after the divorce divorcees are pretty much on their own.

SOME DOCUMENTED VIEWS

Below are extracts from documents provided by some religious organizations outlining policies on divorce and remarriage:

Society of the Church of God in Jamaica

[I]t would be advisable for the church not to actively encourage divorce and remarriage, even in the face of scriptural injunctions, but allow the peculiarity of individual situations to dictate the believer's action.

Given the realities of life, the Church should guard against a judgmental attitude. Persons who for one reason or another find themselves in this position should not be treated as outcasts. Final judgment remains only with God. The Church should do everything possible to counsel the persons facing the possibility of divorce and remarriage. The Church should also allow room for individuals to make their decisions after much prayerful counsel with them, in light of the Church's public policy. The Church should lovingly respect whatever decisions the affected person makes.

Christian believers, who divorce and remarry for reasons permitted by the Bible, should continue to hold offices in the Church. Those who divorce and remarry for other reasons would be subject to the decisions of the local fellowship as to whether or not they can continue to hold office. The Pastor within the Church can also refrain from doing a remarriage, or can do it based on his own Christian conviction following counseling of the party. ("Society of the Church of God in Jamaica," Divorce and Remarriage [Policy Document] Montego Bay. 2004)

Associated Gospel Assembly
In support of societal order, the Scripture takes into account the hardness of the human heart (Matt. 19:8), and so seeks to regulate matters of divorce and remarriage, while acknowledging that this is not God's supreme will for mankind. Marriage officers in the Associated Gospel Assemblies will exercise considered judgment in examining cases concerning divorced persons who apply to be married again. Each marriage officer will personally decide whether there is scriptural ground to consider remarriage in pertinent cases presented to him. AGA affirms for denominational expediency, persons divorced and remarried are not to be elected or remain as pastors or elders of any church (Mark 10:2-12; Matt. 5:31-32; 1 Tim. 3:1-13; Titus 1:5-9). ("Associated Gospel Assemblies," Constitution With By-Laws and Procedures, p.19. Kingston. 2003).

Assemblies of God in Jamaica
The strong feeling of the church against divorce grows out of the clear statement in the Bible that God hates divorce (Malachi 2:16) and that no human being should separate two persons joined together in holy matrimony (Matt. 19:6). Yet the reality of divorce forces the church to draw from Scripture guidelines for instances when God's ideal are not maintained.

In the first case, where husband and wife are professing Christians, neither party is ever to seek a divorce (1 Cor. 7:10, 11). In the second case (mixed marriage), the Christian husband or wife should never initiate or seek a divorce from an unbelieving spouse (1 Cor. 7:12-14). There are only two exceptions that allow for this initiative. A Christian may divorce a spouse only when his/her partner is repeatedly committing the sin of adultery (Matt. 5:32; 19:9).

Under what conditions then may remarriage take place? Jesus taught that if a divorce occurs under a biblical exception as stated earlier, one is free to remarry. In other words, one who has been divorced because of the repeated adultery of a partner (Matt. 5:32; 19:9) is not bound by the former marriage and is free to remarry. The exception clause ("except for marital unfaithfulness") refers to a continuing lifestyle of sexual immorality, not necessarily a single act. Wherever possible, sexually immoral practices should be dealt with through repentance, confession, forgiveness, and reconciliation, thus saving the marriage. In no case does Jesus command divorce when unfaithfulness has occurred; He simply allows it. Nor did Jesus command remarriage when divorce has occurred. However, from Matthew 19:9 it seems that Jesus understood that the divorced will often remarry. Remarriage, like the first marriage, should be "in the Lord" (with a Christian).

The second exception for the remarriage of a divorced person is found in 1 Corinthians 7:15. When an unbelieving spouse is unwilling to remain in the marriage and initiates a divorce, the believer is set free from the marriage and can remarry if he or she chooses without committing adultery.

Another concern has to do with the effect of divorce and remarriage upon the qualifications of those who would serve as pastors, ministers, elders, and deacons. Leaders are held to a high biblical standard.

They are to conform to the requirement that they shall be "the husband of one wife" (1 Timothy 3:2, 12). ...The Assemblies of God believes pastors and church leaders should be those who have not been the guilty party in initiating a divorce. In situations where ministers are the unwilling recipients of divorce they are not to remarry because of their role as moral examples. ("Assemblies of God in Jamaica," [position paper] Divorce and Remarriage, Kingston. 1973).

The Salvation Army

The Salvation Army asserts That God's standard concerning marriage, revealed in Scripture, pertains to all people everywhere. Jesus taught that divorce is failure (Mark 10:2-12; Matthew 19:3-12). Salvationists believe, however, that Jesus' attitude to those caught up in marital strife would never be anything but loving and compassionate.

Therefore, the Salvation Army, while defending vigorously the ongoing relevance of God's will for men and women in relation to marriage, recognizes the reality that some marriages fail and is willing, under God, to offer counsel and succor to couples so affected. Where remarriage could lead to the healing of emotional wounds, the Army will permit its officers to perform a marriage ceremony for a divorced person. Sound doctrine and practical mercy are the hallmarks of the Salvationist's approach to marital and emotional strife.

The Salvation Army reasserts that the strengthening and encouragement of the institution of marriage remains an essential precondition for sound family life which is, in turn, crucial to a stable society. ("The Salvation Army." [Policy Statement] Approved by International Head-quarters, February 1983. Communicated to the author in Montego Bay, Jamaica, May 21, 2005).

General Information
One pastor reported he withheld his divorce status from his denomination because of the repercussions. He has since remarried and continues to keep his past a secret; if his denomination were to find out about his past he could no longer serve as pastor. Another reported that a member of one church, having lost interest in his marriage, inveigled his best friend to enter into a relationship with his wife so he could have a legitimate reason to cop out of the marriage. The plot worked. The friend got involved with the man's wife and did manage to sleep with her, thereby providing 'just' cause for a divorce. All reported being victimized in some way because of divorce. It is to be noted that what is said in a public document or policy statement by a religious organization does not necessarily reflects what obtains on the ground.

In many churches, people experiencing marital dysfunction are caught between a rock and a hard place: if divorced, they are treated as second-class Christians, and if remarried their rating drops to third. Yet while contemplating to divorce or not to divorce their unfaithful spouses are being rewarded and encouraged even, because wedlock is deadlock.

Members of the clergy are not exempted. According to some denominations, divorce and remarriage disqualify a person from pastoral office. In this regard, the words of Swindoll (1977, pp.16, 17) are most appropriate. He stated:

> *Take an honest look at men and women whom God used in spite of their past! Abraham, founder of Israel and tagged 'the friend of God,' was once a worshipper of idols. Joseph had a prison record but later became prime minister of Egypt. Moses was a murderer, but later became the one who delivered his nation from the slavery of Pharoah. Jepthah was an illegitimate child who ran around with a tough bunch of hoods before he was chosen*

by God to become His personal representative. Rahab was a harlot in the streets of Jericho but was later used in such a mighty way that God listed her among the members of His hall of fame in Hebrews 11.

Still unconvinced? There's more. Eli and Samuel were both poor, inconsistent fathers but proved to be strong men in God's hand regardless. Jonah and John Mark were missionaries who ran away from hardship like cowards but were ever so profitable later on. Peter openly denied the Lord and cursed Him, only to return and become God's choicest spokesman among the early years of the infant church. Paul was so hard and vicious in his early life the disciples and apostles refused to believe he'd actually become a Christian – but you know how greatly God used him. We could go on and on. The fi les of heaven are filled with stories of redeemed, refitted renegades and rebels.

The research findings beg the following questions: Why is it that the divorced and remarried are treated so contemptuously in some churches? Why does the Church shoot the wounded in the marriage wars? What happened to Christian compassion for the abused? Why is unfaithfulness rewarded by forcing some people to remain in a bad relationship? Assuming that divorce is a sin, why are divorcees being asked to pay penance if the blood of Jesus cleanses from **all sins**?

3

Commonly-held Interpretations of Scripture

Because the Church factors prominently in the socialization of a significant number of people, including informing perceptions and attitudes toward divorce and remarriage, reflection on some of the biblical issues is a virtual necessity. In this chapter, therefore, an attempt will be made to reflect more profoundly on some of the commonly-held interpretations of Scripture regarding the issues.

God hates divorce
Attitudes toward divorce and remarriage are sometimes based on the Church's interpretation of Malachi 2:16: *"I hate divorce," says the Lord God of Israel, "and I hate a man's covering himself with violence as well as with his garment,"* *says the Lord Almighty*...(NIV).

Unfortunately, some Christians have a difficulty in hating the sin and not hating the sinner. They presume incorrectly that since God hates divorce, divorcees have committed the unpardonable sin and should be shunned. Interestingly, if divorce is always sinful, divorce is not the only sin that God hates; for in the said reference quoted above, we see quite clearly that God hates violence as well. Yet, in the Church, violent people are not treated in the same manner as divorcees. In fact, violent people can get away with murder.

Albeit, there are several other sins that God hates:

> *There are six things the Lord hates, seven that are detestable to Him: haughty eyes, a lying tongue, hands that shed innocent blood, a heart that devises wicked schemes, feet that are quick to rush into evil, a false witness who pours out lies and a man who stirs up dissension*
> *among brothers* (Prov. 6:16-19 NIV).

It is to be noted that the above list of sins it not exhaustive, and as such does not comprise all the sins that God hates. Yet, as brief as this list is, it makes everyone out to be on God's hate or hit list, according to some people. Moreover, since we are all guilty of sin, (which God hates) none of us is really qualified to judge the other. In addition, assuming that divorce is always sinful, since the blood of Jesus cleanses from **all** sin (1 John 1:7), why divorcees should be singled out for special treatment defies logic. It is reasonable to infer then that the current judgmental attitude of sections of the Church toward the divorced and remarried is hypocritical, and demonstrates ignorance concerning God's grace.

Man should not separate what God has joined
Many religious organizations also base their attitude toward divorce and remarriage on their interpretation of the biblical injunction: *what God has joined together let man not separate* (Matt. 19:6 NIV). According to them, since marriage is a sacred act, a person should not divorce under any circumstance whatsoever. In other words, no one has a right to separate what God has joined; and, if divorced, one should never remarry.

Our first task in respect to interpreting this injunction is to ascertain what the Scripture means by *what God has joined together*. What does *join together* means? Does it mean the choosing of a life partner for the unmarried? And if so, how does God go about joining single people together in marriage? If we accept that it is God who joins every married couple together, then all married couples are necessarily right for each other. God cannot do anything that is wrong, can He? Therefore, no matter what the couple is experiencing they should remain in that situation. The God who put them together will work it out, however long it may take: literally, *Till death do us part.*

The reality of life's experience, however, does not support this view. We all know couples whom we knew were not meant for each other. We could also predict with a fair amount of accuracy that their marriage would not last. Was it God who joined them together?

Is God in the business of arranging marriages?
Marriage is that which God has ordained or instituted, but the extent to which He is involved in arranging marriages in heaven is quite debatable. What we know for sure is that God instituted marriage and is a witness to the fact. Because it takes two to make a marriage, two people must come together to form a union. God is not necessarily involved in the choice of a partner, is He? As far as the choice of a partner for marriage goes, what we have in Scripture are broad guidelines. The specifics are left for people to work out for themselves.

The biblical instructions are clear: A marriage involves a congenital (male-female) relationship (Genesis 2:18-25; Matt.19:4, 5); and a Christian marriage should involve two people who are Christians (1 Cor.7:39).

Notice that in the choice of a mate, no mention is made of race or culture. The grounds are moral and religious. Values transcend race and culture, and are underpinned by religion, more specifically—a personal relationship with God. It is important that the couple has shared values and that they are pulling in the same direction, spiritually. This is crucial as the God who created humanity is the One who created marriage as the medium for reproduction and the means of raising up godly seed in the earth(Mal.2:15). Besides addressing one's need for companionship, marriage and the family provides the foundation for addressing other issues, including reproduction, societal, moral and spiritual issues. The theory is if parents are godly, the children of the marriage would be raised to be godly; they should promote godliness and thus honour or glorify the Creator in the world.

As mankind exists, in the main, to glorify God, God is particularly concerned about the character of the people we marry, hence the admonition to the people of God not to be unequally yoked together with unbelievers or pagans (2 Cor. 6:14-15). If couples are not pulling together morally and spiritually, the health of the institution of marriage along with the well-being of those involved will be compromised.

It is apparent that two people must be pulling in the same direction for the marriage to work. Yet there are other ways besides religion, which may make even a Christian couple incompatible or unequally yoked. Moreover, not everyone who makes claim to Christianity is godly or necessarily makes a good candidate for marriage to any or every believer. I do believe that God does and can bring people together in marriage. But in the main God does not go about tying the knot between individuals specially chosen by Him as if their match were made in heaven.

Marriage is entered into by choice
God has given us a brain and the autonomy to make wise choices. The responsibility for the choice of a marriage partner has always been that of the couple. It is the couple who choose for themselves whom to marry. Some people may seek wisdom and God's direction in the matter, but most are influenced by biological, financial and/or emotional considerations, or by *falling in love*. Some indeed fall in love with the wrong person; yet, knowingly and unknowingly they do get married anyway. In all honesty, though, many couples cannot truthfully say that they were joined together with the "right" person, or for the "right" reason/s, or by God. In fact, some would say *the Devil made me do it*.

COMMONLY-HELD INTERPRETATIONS OF SCRIPTURE

God has joined couples together in the sense that it is God who instituted marriage. But generally speaking, marriage is a product of the exercise of a couple's free will. The marriage eclipses God's will insofar as marriage fulfils the Divine will for conjugal relationships, for the propagation of humankind on the earth and for social order. Therefore, once married, a couple should not be separated; for marriage speaks to a special kind of intimacy – and one which is intended to be for life.

As such, the injunction of Jesus, w*hat God has joined together let man not separate*, first of all treats with the issues of divorce and remarriage insofar as they affect the integrity of marriage; it is a terse reminder of the kind of regard we should have for what God has instituted. Secondly, the injunction speaks to the kind of regard we should have for the people that are impacted by the institution, the need for wholeness in the relationship, and the need for marriage partners to be faithful to each other.

Everything, however, must be taken in proper context. Accordingly, we must ask ourselves: what are the circumstances under which Jesus is giving this injunction. An examination of the context reveals that Jesus is responding to the question: *Is it right for a man to divorce his wife for any and every reason.* Note that the real issue taken to Jesus is not divorce *per se*, but the legitimate ground/s on which a man may divorce his wife. In Jesus' day, there were two schools of thought. Both schools commonly accepted adultery as a basis for divorce, but they were divided as to whether there were other grounds as well. One school, the disciples of Hillel, believed a man may put away his wife *for every and any reason*. The other, the disciples of Shemmai, believed that he may do so only on the ground of adultery.

Some theologians argue that divorce was only allowed during the betrothal period. That is, during the so-called period of engagement and before the consummation of the marriage. But this is disputed in Deuteronomy 24:1-4 and John 4:1-17 where the divorcee is seen to have had multiple husbands or have divorced and remarried several times. Moreover, the same penalty prescribed for the adulterer who breaks her vows during the betrothal period is the same prescribed for an unfaithful spouse who breaks her vows after the consummation of the marriage (Deut. 22:22-24). Of note is the fact that in those days the only legal part of the marriage was the betrothal. The act of unfaithfulness before the consummation of the marriage was no less reprehensible than one committed afterwards, and therefore was not treated any differently.

The teachings of the Old Testament allowed divorce on the grounds of *neglect* (Exodus 21:10-11) and *something displeasing* (Deut. 24:1-4). The misinterpretation of this latter provision of divorce, for *something displeasing*, became a constant source of dispute among the Jews. As mentioned above, scholars took extreme positions on the matter. Thus the uncertainty in regard to the limitations of the law served to compromise the integrity of marriage. Apparently, by the time of the New Testament the penalty for adultery, capital punishment (Deut. 22:22-24), was not rigidly enforced. Had it been, there would have been no need for divorce on the ground of adultery since the marriage would have been literally terminated at the death of the offending spouse.

Clearly, Jesus did not encourage the death penalty. In His treatment with the woman taken in adultery, and in the discourse found in Matthew 19, He prescribes divorce. It is also apparent that Moses' Law did not include adultery as a ground for divorce, for it is more than likely under the Old Testament dispensation that the death penalty would have been rigidly enforced. The death penalty being applied would have made no room for divorce because of adultery. As such, the question posed Jesus in the New Testament as to why Moses permitted it (assuming adultery was the only solid ground for divorce) would have been redundant.

In responding to the question, however, it is to be noted that Jesus is pointing His audience to the purpose of God in marriage and is admonishing them to fulfill that purpose, which means honouring one's marital vows. Therefore, Jesus' declaration should not be taken to mean absolutely *no divorce*, for He Himself allows it for adultery. This is clearly stated in the said conversation. Jesus' emphasis is on the intended permanence of marriage, and on maintaining the integrity of the institution, which *God has joined together.*

Without siding with one group or the other, Jesus addresses the real problem – the need at the time to protect the innocent and to uphold the integrity of marriage. Consequently, He does not express any disagreement with Moses' Law, found in Deuteronomy 24:1-4. Instead, Jesus offers an explanation for it – one that recognizes *the heart of the matter to be the matter of the heart. Jesus replied, 'Moses permitted you to divorce your wives because your hearts were hard. But it was not this way from the beginning'* (Matt. 19:8 NIV).

A hard heart is one that is calloused, sinful or spiritually insensitive – one that is inclined to disobey God. Thus our sinful heart affects us in ways that causes us to fall short in attaining God's ideal: *For all have sinned and come short of the glory of God* (Romans 3:23 NIV). Apparently, Moses made a concession in allowing divorce in instances of hardheartedness or sinfulness in order to protect the innocent.

Sin affects God's ideal for marriage
According to Jesus, Moses' reflection on the matter of divorce reveals that God's ideal for marriage as a lifetime commitment is affected by humankind's sinful nature or hardheartedness. The truth is: our sinful nature inclines us to sometimes make the wrong choice in the spouse we choose and in spouses acting inappropriately toward one another. For these and other reasons, the viability of marriages is affected. Any reflection on the divorce issue, must therefore take into account human sinful nature or sinfulness, the need to protect the innocent, and the need to uphold the integrity of marriage.

The integrity of marriage should be preserved, but not at the expense of preserving the integrity or wholeness of the people in it. Nor should the death of a marriage mean the death of a spouse physically, spiritually, psychologically or socially. In His discourse with the scribes and Pharisees, Jesus beckons His audience to look beyond Moses' permission – to recognize the reason for it and to balance that with God's ideal for married partners.

Indeed, God's ideal is *no divorce*, but once sin entered into the human landscape, it changed the picture: not in terms of changing God's ideal, but in terms of our ability to attain the ideal in the real world of sinfulness; and in terms of what God will allow or permit. In a world where sin is an inescapable reality, sinfulness makes it impossible for some people to attain God's ideal or His perfect will for marriage. Failing that, God is gracious enough to avail them His permissive will.

Moses saw fit to permit divorce, because if he did not permit divorce many women would have suffered untold damages at the hand of their hard-hearted husbands and the institution of marriage suffer ill-repute. Paul allowed it, because if a partner no longer wishes the relationship, there is no point in holding on to something that for all practical purposes no longer subsists, or in which there is no mutual interest (1 Cor. 7).

Where hard-heartedness is manifest in the violation of one's vows, or in the death of a marriage, or a partner is determined to divorce or put away his/her spouse for reasons that are less than honourable, the very least a leader can do is to do some damage control. This seems to be the view of Moses in addressing the issue of divorce between 'members of the family of God' (Deut. 24), and the view of Paul in relation to people who are unequally yoked (1 Cor. 7).

During the time of Jesus (and before) there was a preponderance of abuse of innocent female spouses, culminating in divorce. Jesus responds to this by drawing His audience's attention to God's purpose for married couples. Since the integrity of marriage was being compromised, it is understandable that Jesus would emphasize to his audience the need to fulfill God's purpose in marriage. Jesus is therefore not saying "No divorce." He is simply saying that married couples should honour their vows.

Part of Jesus' response to the flippant manner in which divorces were taking place, includes drawing attention to the Jews commonly-held belief in adultery as a just cause for divorce. In doing so, however, Jesus expands the meaning of adultery from the narrow definition of illicit sex to include the willful and unreasonably putting away of a spouse.

Unfaithfulness in marriage is not restricted to adultery
Adultery, as an act of unfaithfulness, is a valid reason for divorce; but according to Jesus, divorce can also be an adulterous act when the basis for the divorce is frivolous. Jesus implies that, if the sole reason for the divorce is so that you may marry another person who has caught your eye, you have committed adultery: *I tell you that anyone who divorces his wife, except for marital unfaithfulness, and marries another woman commits adultery* (Matt. 19:9 NIV).

It is apparent that Jesus' exception clause does not restrict the meaning of marital unfaithfulness to fornication or sexual immorality; nor does the tone of the conversation seek to override other provisions in the Levitical Law (Exodus 21:7-11) and the law of Moses (Deut. 24:1-4), and later Paul's provision of desertion (1 Cor. 7).

Motive is a crucial factor to consider
In drawing our attention to the motive behind divorce, however, Jesus includes a crucial factor to be considered in the mix – that of a person's motive or reason for seeking a divorce. In this expanded definition of adultery, Jesus turns the table on those who came to test Him, and accuses them of unfaithfulness. By so doing, He also provides increased insight into what constitutes adultery and on the issues of divorce and remarriage.

Some translators confuse the issue
However, while Jesus clarifies the issues of divorce and re-

marriage, the translators of Matthew confuse them by the imposition of the phrase, *and whoso marrieth her which is put away doth commit adultery*, into the biblical text (Matt. 19:9 KJV). Consequently, they ridiculously accuse an innocently divorced woman of committing adultery (a sin committed against her), and prior to her being remarried at that; her husband as well being presumed guilty of committing the same sin for having married a divorced woman.

The phrase heretofore mentioned, does not appear in any other translation of the Bible. The Amplified Bible (AB) records it but recognizes it as an interpolation. The New International Version (NIV) and the New American Standard Bible (NASB) do not record it as part of Matthew's gospel. In fact, that phrase cannot be found in the original manuscripts or in the Greek New Testament as being part of Matthew's account of the gospel.

According to Zodhiates (1984), a Greek scholar, a more accurate translation reveals that a person who willfully divorces his wife causes the ex-wife to be stigmatized as having committed adultery and her new husband as well by virtue of his association with her. In order to clarify the matter, Zodhiates invites our appreciation for ancient Jewish culture. He reminds us that in Jewish culture women were regarded as chattels. Viewed as such, they could be divorced at will. Consequently, men were divorcing their wives frivolously – they were divorcing for any and every reason, denying women also a Certificate of Divorce.

Although a divorced woman did not need a Certificate of Divorce to remarry, without a Certificate of Divorce she was presumed guilty of adultery and stigmatized as an adulteress. Her husband shared a similar fate because of his relationship with her. So apart from the injustice of being unreasonably put away, women experienced a further injustice by not being given a Certificate of Divorce by their ex-husband, the absence of which served to impugn their character. They are presumed guilty of adultery and their new husbands presumed to be the culprit with whom they had an affair.

Granting a Certificate of Divorce to a willfully divorced woman did not make the divorce right, but at the very least, she would have been spared the additional injustice of having to wear the stigma of an adulteress and her new husband the stigma of an adulterer. Furthermore, the withholding of a Certificate of Divorce was in violation of Moses' law. Zodhiates believes that Jesus' response also deals with these injustices.

Unfortunately, the mistranslation and subsequent misrepresentation of Jesus, mentioned above, cause many in the Church to believe that a divorcee who is remarried is living in perpetual adultery. But this is clearly not the case.
Dake (1961, p. 46) agrees:

> *He* (Jesus) *did not change the Jewish universal practice that a right to divorce was a right to remarriage. He let this be as it was in Deuteronomy 24:1-4. This is clear from the fact that He referred them to what Moses commanded (v. 3). He did not say that Moses was out of the divine will in making a law of divorce, but merely that it was because of their hardness of heart that such was permitted by God, and that from the beginning this was not the will of God (vv. 6-9).*

Divorcees who remarry are not living in adultery

Dake not only states *that a right to divorce was a right to remarriage*; according to him, the right of remarriage was explicitly stated on the Certificate of Divorce. To support his arguments, he offers proof of what a Certificate of Divorce looked like:

On the ... day of the week ... day of the month ... in the year ... I ... who am also called the son of ... do hereby consent with my own will, being under no restraint, and I do hereby release, send away, and put aside thee, my wife in time past; and thus I do release thee, and send thee away and put thee aside that thou mayest have permission and control over thyself to go to be married to any man that thou mayest desire;

and that no man shall hinder thee from this day forward, and thou art permitted to any man, and this shall be unto thee from me a bill of dismissal, a document of release, and a letter of freedom, according to the law of Moses and Israel. ...the son of ... Witness (ibid).

Some of our theologians, however, such as Chisholm (2003), for example, differentiate between a legal divorce and a spiritual divorce. The argument is: a person can be divorced legally but not divorced spiritually; meaning that, God does not recognize the divorce if there was no legitimate ground for it. The perception is, unless adultery (extramarital sex) is involved, the divorce is not complete; hence the parties are not free to remarry. Advocates of this view believe that only adultery can break the marriage contract.

But we have seen throughout Scripture, that in the matter of divorce, what was recognized according to custom or legally was also recognized spiritually. Where man deviated from the Divine will in the matter of divorce, God in grace acknowledged and even regulated the situation. That is, God permitted divorce in certain cases of hard-heartedness in order to mitigate human suffering and acts of injustice. In Moses' law, for instance, divorce and remarriage is allowed in at least three instances for the same person, on grounds besides adultery (Deut. 24:1-4). We know that the reason could not have been for sexual immorality, because in ancient days a person proven to have committed adultery was stoned to death; hence there was no need for a divorce on the basis of adultery.

God allowed divorce for spiritual adultery
Another case in point is to be found in the book of Ezra. In Ezra 10 we see a troubled nation of Israel coming to terms with their marriages to pagan wives. As a result of the poor choice made in marrying heathen women, lewdness and idolatry became the order of the day. Despite the pain and suffering the divorce would have caused the entire family, Ezra, the priest, saw Israel's separation from their heathen wives an unavoidable solution. Notice that divorce became a

remedy, not for physical adultery, but for spiritual adultery, and that it was God's people divorcing their wives, whom, it seems, were more than willing to remain in the marriage.

Ezra's divorce policy appears harsh, but he seems justified in light of Israel's role to be a witness to the rest of the world – one which they could not reasonably be expected to fulfill while in such a compromised position. It speaks to the spiritual impact of a marriage on the people of God, a relationship which may be described as spiritually abusive or adulterous; and on a people's ability to survive spiritually, their testimony having been compromised and supplanted by paganism. However, the case in the book of Ezra seems an exceptional one.

In the New Testament, a Christian spouse is not encouraged to divorce a non-Christian spouse on the ground of being unequally yoked (1 Cor. 7). Albeit, in the Pauline epistle, we need to bear in mind that Paul is simply responding to a particular situation, one which was localized and did not threaten to undermine the spirituality of the person or nation. Accordingly, one cannot help but wonder what Paul's advice would have been today regarding a situation involving serious psychological, spiritual or physical abuse in a marital relationship. Because God is for peace in every relationship, the absence of which makes a marriage untenable, it is quite plausible that a situation in which there are *irreconcilable differences* between a couple may provide reasonable grounds for divorce, irrespective of the religious mix of the couple. These scenarios might have very well evoked a different response. Since wedlock was not deadlock for God's people in both the Old and New Testaments, shouldn't Christians today be more open to the possibility of other legitimate grounds for divorce besides those mentioned in the Bible?

Has God ceased to speak to His people since the completion and compilation of the Bible? And what about the role of the Holy Spirit as revealer and teacher of things spiritual? By established Scriptural precedents, we have seen divorce and remarriage permitted on grounds besides adultery. In all cases we have observed that the interest of the victim figures highly in the recommendations or injunctions made by the religious leaders. Yet even so, the offended party was not necessarily obliged to insist on upholding the right to divorce; and the offender was not chained to the marriage against his will, although expected to honour his vows.

It is instructive to note, for example, that although adultery was a commonly accepted ground for divorce, it did not necessarily break a marriage spiritually or legally; yet spiritually, morally and legally it qualified the offender as having breached the marriage covenant and the offended to sue for divorce. As it was then and now is, adultery may provide a legitimate reason for a divorce but it is not necessarily the cause of it, nor the only ground on which a person may "legitimately" seek a divorce.

If extra-marital sex is the only ground for divorce, then the essence of marriage is sexual fidelity. Infidelity, though, as the only legitimate ground for a divorce, opens the floodgate for all kinds of abuses, which may do just as much, if not more harm to the relationship than infidelity itself. Infidelity speaks to more fundamental problems often overlooked in marriages.

Sexual fidelity is only one aspect of a marriage
Although sexual fidelity is a fundamental aspect of a marriage contract, it is only one aspect of the relationship. Understandably, adultery cannot be the only cause for a divorce as there are many ways in which a relationship may be breached and accordingly provide the potential for a divorce. Unfaithfulness may be expressed in a variety of ways, and may be manifested in ways that are just as reprehensible and immoral as adultery. The view that extra-marital sex alone provides the basis for a scriptural divorce reduces marriage to something purely physical. It overlooks the social, emotional and spiritual dimension of a marriage, from which the act of sex derives meaning.

Sex does not make a marriage

Sex does not make a marriage, otherwise sex would not be labeled 'immorality' when engaged in illicitly (1 Cor. 6:12-16). Rightly practiced, it is one of the greatest expressions of intimacy, but it ought not to define the relationship. The emotional and spiritual bonding of the married couple more accurately depicts the marital relationship the Bible talks about in Genesis 2:25. It is no wonder that the Bible describes love as the *perfect bond of unity* (Coloss. 3:14). Sex, in the proper context enhances that unity, but sex is only one expression of love. Before and after the marriage, the married couple must come to terms with other issues that are fundamental to the sustenance of the relationship.

Within the complexities of a marriage relationship, there are issues relating to an individual's emotional, physical, social and spiritual well-being, the abuse of which would constitute a breach of the marriage covenant, and therefore provide the potential for divorce. Therefore, all the issues that facilitate that bonding must be attended to – issues that promote intimacy, the nurturing of the commitment and the pursuit of a common goal. If there is no relationship – social and emotional connection – between the couple, their marriage is a mere formality, and otherwise dead!

While it is important to strive to preserve the marital bond, pastoral counselors should not allow that to shackle us so that we become absolutely insensitive to circumstances that would make it inhumane or irrational for a person to remain in a dysfunctional marriage, or in one that is already dead, and to remarry. In addition, wisdom demands that we do not allow evil persons to use legitimate institutions as a cover to satisfy their baser instincts, to perpetuate their evil designs and to imprison a human soul.

Encourage hope but be careful not to play God

Although it is perfectly in order to pray for a miracle and to expect one, we should be careful how we encourage persons to hold on to a marriage which for all practical purposes no longer subsists; that's a work of the Holy Spirit, not the work of pastors and counselors, or other concerned individuals. Too often well-meaning people try to play God. In using their own experience as a bench-mark for all other relationships, or in presuming that they know what is best for the couple in a troubled marriage, or in presuming that they know the mind of God, some people attempt at manipulation and invariably violate a couple's right to choose for themselves.

It is clear that some couples were not meant to be together. Indeed, God can grant grace so that a bad marriage may become a good one; but the reality is that even good marriages fail sometimes. If the marriage is dysfunctional, however, we have an obligation to fix it, with God's help of course. But there is nothing godly in remaining in a dysfunctional marriage in perpetuity. To do so is to bring the institution of marriage in disrepute. Note, however, that the decision to stay or not to stay in a troubled marriage is that of the couple to make, not the counselor, although advice is perfectly in order.

It is imperative to note that God does not impose His will upon anyone. God gives people liberty to decide. Having decided, we may reap the fruit of having made a good decision or face the consequence of the poor choices we have made. Even so, God persists in seeking our redemption. Like a good parent, God gives people space to mature and learn from life's experiences. And, assuming that sin is involved, or a person obtains an unscriptural divorce, the Bible says: *If we confess our sins, He is faithful and just to forgive us our sins and to purify us from **all unrighteousness*** (1 John 1:9 NIV).

In this vein, we should take careful note that our wise and loving Creator allows people to make their own choices in life. If the choices they make so impact the marital relationship that the institution of marriage is grossly undermined; or if a good marriage have gone bad, God is gracious enough to help the couple overcome the situation. Overcoming the situation may involve a lot of things, including counseling; but it does not exclude a person's liberty to seek a divorce. Divorce may become part of the answer to a situation in which the life or wellness of a member of the union is being severely compromised. Albeit, whatever the nature of the breach, the parties are at liberty to decide whether they are going to work at improving the marriage or dissolve it. A marriage is made on mutual consent and it is maintained the same way. Notice Paul's emphasis on mutual consent as the basis for the sustainability of marriage (1 Cor. 7:12, 13), and that in proper context.

Marriage is not slavery

Fundamental to our understanding of marriage, is the fact that marriage is a covenant relationship; but it is not a one-sided or an unconditional covenant. Marriage is not slavery; it is based on mutual consent. Since marriage is a mutually consensual relationship, if the relationship is dead or has been significantly breached, the parties are at liberty to decide whether they want to stay married to each other or not. Where there is no desire to reconcile or to close the breach, separation then becomes the only practical thing to do. By divorcing, such a couple is not undermining the institution of marriage – they are refusing to make a mockery of it. The couple is acting responsibly in preventing further harm, in creating the space for wellness and in granting leave to a partner for a more fulfilling relationship with someone else.

Lifelong marriage is God's ideal, but we do not live in an ideal world. Therefore, in a less than ideal world, we must be context-responsive or reality-centered. God's command not to divorce and God's permission of divorce is a reflection of this practical approach.

The right to divorce is the right to remarry

We may also note that it was commonly accepted by the Jews, including Jesus, that the right to divorce was also the right to remarry. Once a married couple is divorced, there is no further obligation of the parties to each other. A divorced person is free to remarry. This is implied in the conversation with Jesus in Matthew 19, explicitly stated in Moses' instructions on divorce (Deut. 24:1-4) and in Paul's in 1 Corinthians 7. God recognizes the vows taken in marriage and He recognizes the breaking of those vows in divorce as well.

In summary, whereas emphasis of the biblical writers was on sexual immorality, which was deemed to have defiled a spouse, and as such led to the dissolution of the marriage; it is apparent that the writers of the sacred Scriptures, beginning with Moses, did not close their minds to other acts of unfaithfulness which may qualify for a divorce. It is also apparent that the right to divorce was the right to remarriage.

4

Psycho-social Related Issues

The Scriptures, being a fundamental part of our interpretive framework, provide specific references and principles relating to the issues of divorce and remarriage; but religious truth is only one matrix. As all truth being God's truth, other matrices, namely psychology and sociology, are indispensable to a fuller understanding of divorce and remarriage. Moreover, theological positions have practical applications. Accordingly, this chapter seeks to acquaint us with some of the psycho-social related issues that may cause a divorce.

There are many possible causes for divorce. These include: marrying "too early" or "too late," wide differences in age and maturity, differing political persuasions, differences in religion, differences in social class, differences in culture, incompatibility, individualism or selfishness, increased expectations, insensitivity, insufficient knowledge of a spouse, improper or poor communication, infidelity, impracticality, insufficient funds, influx of women into the working world, in-laws, neglect, and societal changes. Any one of these factors or a combination of them may be at the root of marital discord and may lead to divorce.

Marrying 'too early' or 'too late'

There is increased likelihood of persons in their teens failing at marriage, though not necessarily so. Contributing factors include inadequate preparation. They might not have been prepared socially, psychologically or spiritually to cope with as demanding a relationship as marriage. Sometimes, especially in the church, couples did not date long enough to make a wise selection, marry after a short engagement, submit to peer-pressure or pressure from their pastor, and sometimes marry because of pregnancy.

On the other hand, persons who marry late in life, in their forties for example, may be set in their ways, might have grown to be too independent – and this may be the root of frequent disagreements culminating in the erosion of the marriage. It is also possible for couples who marry late in life to have developed communication and social skills, which augur well for individuality and the prevention of enmeshed relationships. Preparation for marriage seems to have more to do with psychology than biology, and increasingly more today with *financology*; that is, financial soundness or thrift. Thus a best age may be hard to factor in the equation of marriage, as maturity does not necessarily come with age, and some would hasten to add that "age is just a number."

Differences in maturity levels and age

Although maturity does not necessarily come with age, wide differences in maturity levels may cause divorce, especially when one partner is too immature. Immaturity is difficult to define; however, for it does not necessarily correspond with chronological or biological age, and has varying degrees of manifestation, even among adults. By and large, it corresponds with an attitude or behavior that is inconsistent with a person with emotional intelligence. Hence one spouse may behave like a child and the other may yield to the temptation to take on the role of mother or father, causing both parties to become disgusted with the anomaly of a parent-spouse relationship. A huge gap, therefore, in maturity levels could make it difficult for the couple to relate to each other as equals or at an adult level and so frustrate the marriage. In addition, the wide disparity in age usually results in significant differences in energy levels, need requirements, comfort levels and expectations, and may result in subsequent misunderstandings and ultimately the breakdown of the union. According to Oates (1996), *Other conflicts can arise. The young and the not-so-young married couple ...may be in a silent power struggle about who is going to dominate whom* (p. 59). Too wide an age gap between the married couple may be a source of disaffection and can lead to the demise of the marriage.

Differing political persuasions
Differing political persuasions can be a source of disaffection and may increase the likelihood of a divorce as well. Spouses who have allegiance to different political parties may very well find themselves in regular feuds over politics. Some people take their politics very seriously (too seriously), so much so that their political loyalties often blur their vision thereby hindering them from seeing the wider picture or from accepting issues on their face value, without attaching some kind of political undertone. This mindset afflicts some people with mental and emotional astigmatism to the extent that their perceptual framework has a difficulty in perceiving and appreciating additional light, or adjusting to other political perspectives. This may be a constant source of conflict and may negatively impact the marriage.

Differences in religion
Negatively impacting marriages is our refusal to adjust our perceptual framework theologically as well. Where there are significant differences in religion, it is highly likely that spouses will frequently 'lock horns' over religious views. But 'locking horns' is not the problem. It is a couples' intolerance of each other's religious persuasion and the differences in lifestyle that their belief systems create.

Religious alliances have deep psychological underpinnings and do not readily acquiesce to, or accommodate contrary views. Seventh Day Adventists, for instance, do not accommodate other religions in terms of their day of worship and any other activity besides worship on a Saturday. Too, some Adventists maintain a strict vegetarian diet and refuse to have anything to do with pork or other forms of meat. Marriage to someone of a different religious persuasion could expose the couple to great stress, especially if the other spouse is equally committed to his/her religion and is intolerant of the religion of his/her spouse.

Jehovah's Witnesses do not celebrate birthdays nor Christmas; neither do they believe in blood transfusion. A Baptist spouse may not appreciate the treating of his/her birthday as if it was just an ordinary day. And in a 'life and death' matter would raise serious objections to any attempt to forbid the giving or receiving of blood. The way Muslims relate to women may pose a problem for a woman who was brought up in Christianity. She may be unwilling to conform to the Muslim tradition and the Muslim may be inclined to enforce obedience. Religious intolerance and religious differences can really destroy a marriage.

However, because of the high value most religions place on the family, it is expected that religious persons would divorce less and that there would be fewer divorces when partners share the same faith. According to Beit-Hallahm and Argyle (1997), divorce is more likely when the partners do not share the same faith, and the difference in religious persuasion has been found sometimes to be one of the strongest predictors of an unsuccessful marriage. However, they also believe that religion is able to reduce the divorce rate of the religious by 50%.

Difference in social class
In some environments, class-consciousness is just as strong as religious consciousness. Big differences in one's social class may pose a serious threat to the viability of a marriage. One party may feel inferior and act out that inferiority in ways that reinforce the devalued self, ultimately leading to the demise of the relationship. On the other hand, feelings of superiority by the other party may result in domineering tendencies and behaviors that are absolutely unacceptable if

the relationship is to survive.

Differences in culture

Huge cultural differences also have the potential to cause dissonance, especially where one party portrays cultural superiority, or disparages that of the other spouse's culture. Nigerian men for example may regard their wives as 'property;' they may subscribe to the cultural practice of polygamy, in the superiority of men and in the inferiority of women. Thus marriage of Nigerian men to Jamaican women, for example, may be tenuous as women in Jamaica would find this situation untenable.

Even within one's own culture there can be a problem, as every culture has its subculture. The way in which things are done in one subculture may be different from that of another, and hence may be a source of discontent. For example, some men may insist that their wives do things the same way they were done by their own parents. This may be as simple a task as food preparation or in the way the toothpaste is squeezed to complex matters as the running of the house or the management of finances. Incompatibility covers a wide spectrum of subjects.

Incompatibility

One of the leading causes of marital dysfunction is incompatibility, otherwise referred to as the "unequal yoke." A couple cannot pull together when there are radical differences, or when they have radically differing outlooks on life. However, if the couple is committed to the relationship and is able to make the psychological adjustment, incompatibility then becomes a welcome challenge. Incompatibility, in and of itself need not result in divorce. Much depends on how committed the couple are to each other, the nature of the differences they face, and their level of spiritual, intellectual, social and emotional intelligence. In fact, "incompatibility" may add another dimension to each spouse's knowledge base, which may indeed broaden a spouse's horizon in a positive way; or, at the very least, add some spice to an otherwise boring relationship. Moreover, what some people shun and regard as incompatibility may be actually embraced by others as *complementarity*. It all depends on perspectives and comfort levels.

Individualism or selfishness

Preoccupation with individualism and self-fulfillment, loss of a community base to support family life, downplaying of the concept and practice of covenant commitment, and emergence of materialism as a dominant value, also cause divorce (Balswick and Balswick, 2003). Huge differences in the value system of a couple may make it difficult for them to 'pull together' or to work as a team. The couple may become so preoccupied in the pursuit of their own objectives that the marriage is relegated to a relationship of convenience. The absence of synergy will impact levels of intimacy, and may ultimately result in a divorce.

Increased and unrealistic expectations

Couples are seeking more fulfilling personal relationships and an improved standard of living. Emphasis is always on 'better.' 'For worse' was never seriously contemplated. Therefore, any form of setback could result in a partner copping out. Stivers, et al (1994), remind us that under Judaism (the religion from which Christianity evolved), women were favoured for their childbearing ability and their willingness to submit to their husbands. Having been sold by their fathers, married women were viewed as chattels and their personhood denied. Being married meant that women became the personal property of their husbands, but love did not necessarily have anything to do with it. There was a cultural understanding that women existed for the good pleasure of their husbands, childbearing being the coveted prize.

This is not so in our post-modern world. A new set of dynamics is now at play. Women are no longer willing to accept child-bearing role as their lot in life, but are demanding more power - more in terms of intellectual, emotional and physical fulfillment, including equality with the masculine gender. Where aspirations are not being attained on account of the marriage, some women may be inclined to seek a divorce.

Also, romanticism of marriage, influenced by Hollywood, may result in unreasonable expectations and subsequent disillusionment. Emphasis on romantic love colors some persons' perception of marriage so that the essence of marriage, to them, is romance and bliss. This romantic illusion causes some women to expect more from their husbands than they are really capable of providing. Consequently, once the reality of marriage subsumes marital bliss, such persons may wish to take flight.

Insensitivity
Lack of awareness and, or unresponsiveness to the needs of a spouse, is potentially damaging to a relationship. It may be the root of resentment by a spouse who may feel neglected or unappreciated. The problem may be exacerbated when the offended spouse fails to communicate clearly and appropriately his/her feelings.

Improper or poor communication
A major cause of dissonance in relationships is improper or poor communication. Insufficient communication or poor communication often causes misunderstandings and mistrusts. It is not unusual for some women to expect their husbands to be mind-readers, while some men seldom communicate with their wives. In addition, some couples lack problem-solving skills hence attack each other instead of the perceived problem/s. This ultimately undermines the relationship, creating discord and emotional distance between them.

Insufficient knowledge of a spouse
Many couples marry without taking time to really know each other. They might have had a short time dating and or a brief engagement. Before even meeting their spouse, they might have been turned on by romantic notions of love and are in too much of a hurry to say, *I do*, only to wish later, *I did not*. And as Jamaicans say: *Si mi an come live wid mi a two different sinting*. Also, some persons enter marriage with emotional 'baggage' or mental illnesses. This too may severely

impact their relationship. If professional help is not received, the situation may persist, and it is quite likely that a partner will want to exit the marriage.

Infidelity
Another cause of distancing is infidelity. Infidelity is sometimes caused by need; other times by greed. Spouses sometimes are unfulfilled sexually; they are frustrated with their partner: sex may be boring or they are not getting enough sex. Appetites may differ where sex is concerned. Unfulfilled partners may seek fulfillment elsewhere. Some spouses do have a larger appetite for sex or an addiction thereto. If the married partner has a difficulty coping, they may engage in extra-marital sex: and once trust is eroded in this way, it becomes very difficult to trust that person again.

However, being unfulfilled sexually is not the only factor that leads to infidelity. The inability or neglect of a man to meet his wife's financial needs may result in her having a "man on the side" to compensate for her husband's "weakness." She may choose to have a "sugar daddy" to help her out financially.

A wife's weakness in nagging her husband can also be a source of infidelity. Women who are constantly complaining or "henpecking" their husbands, for example, sometimes drive them into the arms of other women. For a little peace and quiet, their men may stay away from home for unusually longer periods of time. Coupled with that, their off-work activities may include fraternizing with other women, who appears more calm and sociable. On account of their disaffection at home, men may look to these women for affirmation and friendship instead of to their wives. When people connect emotionally, the friendship may grow into something else. Plus, when uncomfortable at home, men become more vulnerable to the advances of other women, especially women who are more amiable than their wives. The list includes their cooperative, polite and understanding secretaries, personal assistants or colleagues. Once disconnected from their spouses emotionally, physical separation becomes a mere formality afterwards.

Impracticality
Impracticality is another potential source of divorce. Some couples are so impractical that they make unreasonable demands on each other. For example, one spouse may have a difficulty in postponing present wants in order to satisfy present needs, while the other spouse may have a difficulty confusing need with desire. This may be a source of contention and discontent, especially in cases where limited resources are already under pressure.

Insufficient funds
Financial stress has always been a major cause of breakdown in marriages. Lack of financial resources often evokes inappropriate responses. Apart from becoming unfaithful, couples invariably take out their frustrations on each other, and as a result undermine their marriage.

Long hours spent in the working world
Some marriages may also be undermined by the long hours couples spend away from each other at work. The fact that both partners are busy working could affect the quality time couples spend together and so negatively impact the marriage.

In addition, women who enter the working world experience a change in status. Economic independence may cause some women to become more assertive, aggressive even, and feel 'more liberated.' Some women may become less tolerant of marriages that do not quite meet their expectations. The ability to survive without the support of a husband, coupled with being able to find other ways to meet social needs outside a marital relationship, wives today find it easier to cop out of a difficult marriage much more easily than in years gone by.

In-laws
Another way in which a marriage may be impacted negatively is through the meddling of in-laws. Well-meaning in-laws sometimes intervene in the marriage of relatives in an at-

tempt to fix things or to control the relationship of the couple.

> *Relatives of the couple – parents, siblings, uncles, aunts, grandparents – are often told of the difficulty the marriage is in. Often these persons are mature and wise enough to be a catalyst for reconciliation. If this does not happen, the relatives turn supportive of their own kin or pronounce a curse on both partners. In the latter instance, they increase the isolation of the couple. Friends outside the family are often more helpful than kin folks because they can maintain more objectivity* (Oates 1997, p. 61).

The problem is compounded sometimes when a spouse of a troubled marriage solicits the help of in-laws, unilaterally. Apart from the absence of objectivity, by virtue of their family ties to one of the parties, the other party invariably disapproves of in-laws involvement in the marriage and may feel ganged upon.

On the other hand, a couple may take this "one-flesh" relationship so seriously that they abandon their relatives, including their father and mother. Usually, it is one spouse who insists on this level of "separateness," but the couple may become so enmeshed and one's spouse becomes so controlling that he/she suffocates the other. The "suffocation" itself may be a source of marital discord and in time the "separateness" from family may drive a wedge between the couple when the person being separated from his/her family feels strongly enough to change the status quo of the "*out-lawed*" in-laws. Moreover, the couple's isolation generally catches up with them, especially in troubled times when the real value of family support is needed and appreciated.

Nevertheless, some in-laws do contribute to their own distancing, for they may not be sensitive enough to allow the married couple space to live their own lives. They constantly invade the couple's privacy or may be too present in their day-to-day affairs for the in-laws to be appreciative of them.

Thus in-laws may play a disruptive role in a marriage if boundaries are not clearly defined and respected. The often-mentioned case of the meddling mother-in-law cannot be overstated.

Inattentiveness or neglect
It cannot be overstated either for one to be careful not to neglect his/her spouse. There are many things that can cause spouses to be sidetracked from each other, leading to neglect. The birth of children into a family, for example, can be a source of tremendous blessing or a source of marital disaffection.

It is not unusual for a mother to center her life on the children to whom she has given birth and whom she adores. Consequently, her role as wife becomes overshadowed or displaced by her role as mother, so much so that the husband's needs are neglected. In light of this, the neglected husband may seek attention elsewhere or embrace that which is dispensed toward him by a coworker, colleague or friend. This invariably leads to infidelity. In addition, a spouse may be so immersed in study or career, and even church activities that a partner may experience neglect. It is so easy for couples to take each other for granted. No matter how solid the relationship may be at first, if it is not nurtured it will eventually die.

Societal changes
Other explanations for marital disaffection include the decline of certain barriers, which traditionally had discouraged divorce. Citing Lewis and Spanier, Balswick and Balswick (1999) stated:

1. *Religious doctrine and norms have been liberalized to permit the possibility of divorce in a difficult marriage.*
2. *External pressures against and the external stigma of divorce has decreased; correspondingly, tolerance for divorce has increased.*
3. *Societal norms stressing commitment and obligation have eased.*

4. *Liberalization of divorce laws and the availability of legal aid make it easier for persons contemplating divorce to actually follow through.*
5. *Alternatives to one's present spouse become manifest as males and females increasingly work and socialize together. The redefinition of gender roles has resulted in wives being less economically dependent upon husbands, and husbands being less emotionally dependent upon wives* (p. 310).

Having examined some of the psycho-social factors that may cause a divorce, we may now look at some of the psycho-social affects of divorce.

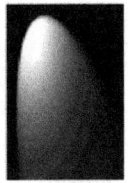

5

Consequences of Separation

On divorcee-spouse
Dobson (1997) gives an interesting excerpt from an article in *Atlanta Magazine,* written by Pat Conroy, entitled "Death of a Marriage." Conroy's article graphically depicts the emotional trauma many divorcees experience. Below is an extract from Dobson's excerpt.

> *Each divorce is the death of a small civilization. Two people declare war on each other, and their screams and tears infect their entire world with the bacilli of their pain. The greatest comes from the wound where love once issued forth. I find it hard to believe how many people now get divorced, how many submit to such extraordinary pain; for there are no clean divorces. Divorces should be conducted in abattoirs or surgical wards. In my own case, I think it would have been easier if Barbara had died. I would have been gallant at her funeral and shed real tears – far easier than staring across a table, telling each other it was over. It was a killing thing to look at the mother of my children and know that we would not be together for the rest of our lives. It was terrifying to say good-bye, to reject a part of my own history.*

When I went through my divorce I saw it as a country, and it was treeless, airless; there were no furloughs and no holidays. I entered without passport, without directions and absolutely alone. Insanity and hopelessness grew in that land like vast orchards of malignant fruit. I do not know the precise day that I arrived in that country. Nor am I certain that you can renounce your citizenship there. Each divorce has its own metaphors that grow out of the dying marriage. One man was inordinately proud of his aquarium. He left his wife two weeks after the birth of their son. What visitors noticed next was that she was not taking care of the aquarium. The fish began dying. Two endings became linked in mind. For a long time I could not discover my own metaphor of loss – until the death of our dog, Beau, became the irrefutable message that Barbara and I were finished.

Beau was a feisty, crotchety dachshund Barbara had owned when we married. It took a year of pained toleration for us to form our alliance. But Beau had one of those illuminating inner lives that only lovers of dogs can understand. He had a genius for companionship. To be licked by Beau when you awoke in the morning was a fine thing.

On one of the first days of our separation, when I went to the house to get some clothes, my youngest daughter, Megan, ran out to tell me that Beau had been hit by a car and taken to the animal clinic. I raced there and found Ruth Tyree, Beau's veterinarian. She carried Beau in to see me and laid him on the examining table. I had not cried during the terrible breaking away from Barbara. I had told her that I was angry at my inability to cry. Now I came apart completely. It was not weeping, it was screaming, it was despair.

The car had crushed Beau's spine, the X ray showing irreparable damage. Beau looked up at me while Dr. Tyree handed me a piece of paper. I leaned against the examining table and cried as I had never cried in my life, crying not just for Beau but also for Barbara, the children, myself, for the death of a marriage, for inconsolable loss. Dr. Tyree touched me gently, and I heard her crying above me. And Beau, in the last grand gesture of his life, dragged himself the length of the table on his two good legs and began licking the tears as they ran down my face. I had lost my dog and found my metaphor. In the X ray of my dog's crushed spine, I was looking at a portrait of my broken marriage. But there are no metaphors powerful enough to describe the moment when you tell the children about divorce.

Divorces without children are minor league divorces. To look into the eyes of your children and to tell them that you are mutilating their family and changing all their tomorrows is an act of desperate courage that I never want to repeat. It is also their parents' last act of solidarity and the absolute sign that the marriage is over. It felt as though I had doused my entire family with gasoline and struck a match. For a year, I walked around feeling as if I had undergone a lobotomy. There were records that I could not listen to because of their association with Barbara, poems I could not read from books I could not pick up. There is a restaurant I will never return to because it was the scene of an angry argument between us. It was a year when memory was an acid. I began to develop the odd habits of the very lonely. I turned the stereo on as soon as I entered my apartment. I drank to the point of not caring. I cooked elaborate meals for myself, and then could not eat them. I had entered into the dark country of divorce, and for a year I was one of its ruined citizens. I suffered. I survived. I studied my-

self on the edge, and introduced myself to the stranger who lived within.

Like Conroy, divorcees generally experience grief, a sense of loss, guilt, shame and failure. And these negative emotions are reinforced by a society that regards them as failures and the divorce as a sign of divorcees' inadequacy. Support networks may be lost as some persons may be ostracized from their church or families. The attitude of society toward divorce and divorcees adds to the trauma.

Divorce is emotionally disturbing. It sometimes results in shock and disorientation. It is more traumatic when friends and family disapprove, when it comes suddenly, or when one party does not want the divorce, or when one party remains emotionally fused to the ex-partner. Pottinger (1999, p. 13) noted that apart from affecting one's equilibrium, the separation also disrupts interpersonal bonds:

...there is a forced isolation of self and an often subconscious egocentrism or insensitivity to the feelings of others. Such reactions can create bewilderment, confusion, and anger in friends, relatives, and co-workers.

There is also the problem of loneliness and social readjustment. Even if the couple did not get along, at least they provided company for each other. Now that they are separated, they will experience loneliness. The need or desire for sexual fulfillment poses quite a challenge. For the Christian, this is a taboo outside of marriage. Unless severely handicapped or disturbed mentally, however, the average divorcee craves for sex and yearns for an outlet, thereby increasing the pressure to remarry. The pressure to marry becomes even greater in an environment where it is expected that parents should be more moral than non-parent adults.

A change in relationship with one's peers may also factor in the equation. Divorcees new status creates a certain amount of ambiguity – they do not quite fit amongst the unmarried –

and they do not fit with the married either. As a result, divorcees may find that their social circle diminishes. Their married friends may not invite them out as much, since activities generally revolve around couples. In addition, the temptation to take sides may exclude one or the other from the circle. Moreover, divorcees join the ranks of potential alternative spouses for persons already married. Like those who have never been married, they are viewed by spouses as potential threats and are sometimes treated accordingly. Female spouses, especially, are usually very guarded of their relationships and may make unmarried women (even friends) feel uncomfortable when around their spouse. Pressure to build a new life before they are emotionally free from a former spouse adds to divorcees' stress, while the need for companionship is an ever-present reality. In the meantime, as divorcee-women advance in age they become less desirable as the trend is for older men to go for younger women of child-bearing age, a fad that may soon fade away.

On divorcee-parents
Psycho-social effects may manifest in parents sexual acting-out, vengeful deeds against the former spouse, emotional outbursts, periods of depression, or fears and concern about finances. Due to the fact that one person may now have to do the work of two there may be a work overload for the single parent having custody of the children.

There is also a cultural and institutional pressure emanating from the feeling that 'children need both parents.' So the divorcee-mother/father is under constant criticism or advice relating to the importance of acquiring a spouse as surrogate parent for the children. Some parents may never remarry for fear of being hurt again. Mothers may be fearful of bringing a man into the home for fear of incest or child molestation – these are common problems in homes where there are surrogate parents or stepchildren. Men are not as fearful, perhaps because incidences of mothers molesting their surrogate children are not so common.

As the children get older and the reality of the imminent

establishment of their own abode hits home, however, divorcee-parents may become increasingly lonely and worried about being single for the rest of their lives. There is romanticism in the children as well and a perception of kinship structures. As such, children may make demands upon parents to remarry.

When women remarry, their ex-husband's identity may become threatened as father. This may be a real source of stress. In addition, since mothers generally get custody of the children, fathers may experience emotional strain for not seeing them. Furthermore, fathers' relationship with their children may become strained due to custodial rights as visitation rights of fathers are usually restricted, thus limiting time spent with their children. Non-custodial fathers may visit regularly for a while but visits sometimes taper off because of his anger with the system and the ex-wife; plus, contacts with the ex-spouse may become less or undesirable where the ex-spouse has been vindictive.

The tendency of some children to show affection for the divorcee-father only when they want something or have problems may result in fathers suffering from depression. Since men are not overtly expressive emotionally and do not talk as much as women do, the children may buy into the perception that men do not suffer emotionally nor do they have need for care and comfort.

Children are sometimes forced to 'take sides' with the divorcee-mother who has custody of them; and the mother may not countenance or encourage the father's participation in the children's lives save to dole out funds. Consequently, the divorcee-father may take on the image of Santa Claus, except that he is obliged to say "Ho! Ho! Ho!" more frequently and dole out gifts all year round. The image of the Santa Claus father may stay with the children thus affecting their perception of males generally and of fathers in particular.

Essentially, there are four kinds of fathers – the *santafied*, the *sissified*, the *sentified* and the *sirtified*.

The *santafied* father is one whose chief function is that of doling out the money and giving gifts. Although he might be living with his family at home, he is only present physically as he is uninvolved in the home and in the children's lives. He may also be one who has a visiting relationship with his family. Basically, he's not there.

The *sissified* father belongs to a matriarchal household. The wife, the head of the house, is usually the higher income earner or is more educated or smarter. This father may feel intimidated by his wife, or he just simply refuses to assert himself. As a result, he has no say in decision-making. Thus he generally agrees with everything his wife says or, for 'peace sake,' allows her to have her own way; otherwise, he has no voice.

The *sentified* father belongs to a patriarchal household. He is head of his house and rules by 'divine right' – 'for this cause he has been sent.' He is generally authoritarian, strict and overbearing. The wife is usually passively submissive and refers major decisions to him, including disciplining of the children. The roles are clearly defined. He is a good provider.

The *sirtified* father is a well-adjusted, self-assured, respected, confident male who possesses good leadership skills. He is adventuresome and loving and takes active interest in the total well-being of his family. Although he is the recognized head of the house, he shares power with his wife. In this household roles are relatively fluid, are based upon ability, and there is mutual accountability. The *sirtified* father is generally sensitive to his environment.

Because fathers are neither as demonstrative in expressing their pain nor do they overtly present themselves as in need of emotional support as women do, they are more inclined to be forgotten or to be ignored than mothers. The tendency is for men to suffer silently. But although fathers react differently to situations, they are in many respects just as sensitive as mothers and in need of support.

In an article, "Divorced Dads Need Support Too" (The Daily Gleaner, June 12, 2003), according to the writer, from an interview of sixty divorced families in Marian County, California, Judith Wallerstein concluded:

> *Adult children of divorcees were more often angry with their fathers, and 'fathers in divorced families were less likely to enjoy close bonds with their adult children, especially their sons.' This stood in marked contrast to fathers and sons from intact families.*

On grandparents

While divorcee-parents are generally affected negatively by divorce, as part of the wider family network, their own parents and the grandparents of their children do suffer greatly as well. They too experience hurt/pain, a sense of loss, and do grieve over the failed relationship. The closer a parent is to the divorcee-son/daughter, the more traumatic the experience.

Apart from losing a son/daughter-in-law, grandparents may be alienated from their grandchildren by a spiteful divorcee-parent. This can be very disturbing emotionally. The divorce may also be a source of dissonance or resentment between the parents of the divorced as divorcees' parents tend to take sides with their children. Grandparents are sometimes affected economically as well, as divorcees often become unable or less able to support their parents financially due to the weakening of divorcees' financial base. On the other hand, the grandparents may become inconvenienced or experience a strain on personal resources as they may be called upon to assist in providing accommodation or financial assistance to their needy divorcee-family members.

On divorcee-children

Divorce has a wide-ranging effect not only upon adults who make these decisions but also, in particular, upon their children. The psychological and social effects of divorce are illustrated in a short story entitled "Life is Not a Bed of Roses" by an undergrad student while attending the University of the West Indies (UWI). Pottinger (1999, pp. 11-12) records the story.

Life is Not a Bed of Roses

The phrase "life is not a bed of roses" is one big understatement that I have come to understand. People who have minor difficulties use this phrase lightly but I think I should buy the copyright so it would only be used in my situation, as the better part of my youth has been sheer hell.

It all began when my comfortable little world crumbled because the two people I admired and respected most were no longer the loving couple I once knew. They snapped and snapped at each other until the little bit, which was holding them together snapped in two. And that was the end, or should I say the beginning of my life of sheer hell.

The separation of my parents hit me like a ton of bricks! I tried to throw off the awful pain it inflicted upon me by wishing I was young and naïve as my little five-year-old sister. She thought Daddy was not coming home because he had "passed on," which was the only answer Mom could find to give Shauna.

I must admit, the separation affected my Mom severely too. It reached the point where her parenting practices became non-existent. Our once beautiful relationship now turned into that of a forceful slave master and an ill-treated slave. She became totally insensitive to my needs, and I just did not know how to deal with this new monster of a mother.

Anyway, at that time, I could not care less about Mommy's pain. All I could think about was me, and the fact that a fifteen year old did not deserve to have this big messy load shoved down her throat, just when the world was proving to be a wonderful place and Dwight from next door had just started to show a little interest in me. Anyway, might as well he had kept his over-sized nose in the air, as he usually does when he passes me by, because this separation had changed me. It reached the point where one day I knocked a smile off Dwight's face and sent him flying in a pool of water with his nose right back in the air. I just could not understand why he was so bright and chirpy with this beaming smile as if life was a bowl of strawberry ice cream. As far as I was concerned, life was the pits, so the comprehension of his mood was totally beyond me.

It is all well and good for you to sit there and say, "Poor Dwight, he did not deserve that;" but what about me? After all, it was I who had to rush home to collect my sister from school and cook dinner because Mom was holding down two jobs in order to keep us alive. Not to mention the fact that the cleaning and washing automatically became my duties because my now disgusting Mom says she now foot the bills so I had better play my part. This was very hard for me, especially when I thought about the fact that I should be out there living it up with my friends. Instead I was struggling with all this household work like an old maid.

I must admit that by now I did not have many friends since the likes of me just could not stand to hear them bragging about their perfect little mummies and daddies. Eventually, I detached myself from my peers and trod slowly in my now one-man gang. Even until this day I am still anti-social and full of anger and pain. But it no longer affects Dwight from next door. It now affects Paul. Dear sweet Paul who loves me so much and wishes to marry me. But I just cannot relate to him properly, not to mention marrying him. I will not give this divorce thing a chance to hit me directly. Oh no! I have had my fair share.

There is another thing. Paul just chats on and on about his happy childhood. He is ignorant of mine because of my choice to keep it to myself. Still, I hate him for it. Although I should not, I cannot help it. That is just me, bitter, bitter as a gall.

Looking back now I can say there was a little good that came out of the separation. When Dad began visiting, he would shower me with love and attention and not to mention money. In the long run, however, that was no good because the attention did not ease the pain or remove the keloids left by the terrible wounds of having my heart torn apart. Even the money was no fun after a while. Can you believe that? Well you see there were no friends to blow it with. Wow! What can I say? Life is certainly no bed of roses. Trust me.

It is true that *"life is no bed of roses"* for children of divorced parents. As described above, divorce sets off a series of intra-relational and inter-relational wounds that may affect a child for years to come. Psycho-social effects are relative to the ages of children or to the development stage of each child. Young children are more negatively affected than older ones. Moreover, children react differently to the same stimulus. How each child copes will depend on the age of the child at the time of the divorce, on the child's coping skills and on the support systems in place to cushion the blow or loss.

The absence of a father or mother from the home will result in grief, especially for the children. They will mourn the loss because that person was part of a structure – the only one known to them. This in turn will result in uncertainties and corresponding insecurities. The normal world of the children is disturbed and things will be different.

Differences in family structure, however, need not have a negative impact. In fact, if properly managed, the differences may open new doors for growth and unleash possibilities that were before hindered or unrecognized. Nuclear families are not necessarily better than divorced families. The nuclear family and the divorcee-family both have the potential for dysfunction or health. What is important is that the family is functional, appropriately adapting to changes – facilitating an environment of nurture and care – helping each member toward growth and development.

Divorce does not necessarily cause child delinquency. Child delinquency is usually a result of family conflicts, which may be present in both the nuclear family and the divorcee-family. Granted, the absence of a parent does cause additional strain, but how divorcees manage the factors accompanying divorce is the overarching challenge

Factors that accompany divorce are variables which may contribute more to delinquency than the divorce itself. For example, the divorcee-father may have difficulty maintaining two homes, especially if he has since remarried; the divorcee-mother may have to reduce her standard of living – may have less for food, less for education, and housing, etc. Children of divorced parents may be forced to live in poverty and in areas where crime rates are high. In situations where mothers have to go out to work, children may be left unsupervised, thereby making them more susceptible to negative elements in their environment – all of these affect children more psychologically.

The absence of one partner may retard their progress as children. They may lose confidence in themselves and become reluctant to experiment. They may also lose out on the benefits of the combined resources of parents. On the other hand, in the ideal family, children benefit from the strength and security of both parents. And they are free to experiment, to assume greater levels of independence and responsibility knowing that if they fail their parents are there to provide encouragement and a safety net.

Assuming that the marriage is a good one, when it remains intact it provides safety, a sense of identity and belonging, thereby providing a firm ground for trusting others. Rupturing of the structure shakes the children's identity, allowing fear to creep in and undermine their development. When the marriage is a bad one, depending on how the divorce is managed, divorce may lead to greater levels of family dysfunction or the family may experience improvement and growth.

The sacrifice of a problem member may actually lead to the saving of the others. It is possible too that the children may take on responsibilities much earlier and mature much faster knowing that they have to look more inwardly for strength to cope with life's vicissitudes. However, while divorce may render some children better-off, majority evidence has shown that divorce affects most children adversely. Balswick and Balswick agree with the findings of Walswick and Kelly (1980) that *long after the divorce children have a pervasive fear of being disappointed, betrayed, or abandoned, even if caring and loving relationships are maintained with each parent.*

Children are affected in other ways as well. Children sometimes idolize the missing parent and often blame the present partner for the loss of the other. There is also the tendency of children to blame self for the break-up of the relationship. Fantasies and intense yearning to re-establish the family unit can also pose a problem. They may display certain negative behaviours or internalize their problems because they feel powerless to change the divorce situation. Unfortunately, parents are usually not available to help them adjust emotionally because they are too busy taking care of their survival needs.

Single parents' busyness in order to provide for the children sometimes prevents the parent from giving them adequate attention or affection, television sometimes doing most of the parenting. In addition, instead of overt signs of affection, some parents lavish their kids with overt signs of affluence. Invariably, this is overcompensation for their lack of attentiveness and for what they themselves did not receive while growing up as children. Lack of supervision, permissiveness and overcompensation by way of material indulgence and so on, do have a negative impact on children's values and attitudes. For example, it may cause them to grow up equating love with things, becoming 'spoilt' or indiscipline, and lacking in thrift.

Parents bad attitudes or negative feelings are sometimes unwittingly transferred to kids. When parents do not feel good and positive about themselves, negative feelings affect their children. Anxiety levels of children increase when they succeed in playing off one parent against the other. Although children do this to get away with more, it frightens them when they realize their parents lack coordination and are not sufficiently in charge. As a result instability increases and the behaviour of children worsens.

Oates (1997) noted:

> *Some adolescents who were previously very talkative and spontaneous become guarded and minimal in their conversation with adults...Second, money often become scarcer, and these teenagers may manipulate other adults in the family for money. At worst, they may steal from relatives. These two behaviours may be rooted in basic distrust of adults... They mourn within themselves and look out for their own survival* (p. 38)

Embittered by the divorce, some mothers force their children, especially their daughters, to hate their fathers. Daughters' awareness of their dependence on their mothers for survival may cause them to form an alliance, which projects mother as always right and father as always wrong. As a result, daughters may make an unhealthy bargain to always love, help and defend their mother so she too won't leave them. They are trapped in the dilemma to ignore their own needs in order to be Mommy's best friend and protector.

Some parents may punish a child for things they see in themselves or the ex-spouse. They may take out their frustration on the child; some children may even experience hate simply because they remind the parent of the ex- spouse.

Absence of a father or an appropriate male figure in the life of a female child may affect her relationship with men in later life. Research done in America and England show that teenage girls from single parent homes without fathers become sexually active earlier and are more likely to get pregnant. New Zealand Psychologist, Bruce Ellis and his team, studied 7,000 girls from pre-school to age 18. Ellis, *et al* found that teenage girls raised without fathers were more likely to suffer from depression, drop out of school and have other behavioural problems.

Teenage girls generally have difficulty interacting with other men, although they desire and seek out male attention. When fathers are not present in the home or do not express love for their girls, they may grow up with a low self-esteem. Having been starved of a male figure, feelings of insecurity may cause them to cling to the first man that shows them some attention. They might not truly love the man but cling to him nevertheless. In addition, they may become over jealous and possessive, suffocating the spouse, who eventually leaves them anyway.

Secunda (1992) posits that girls have a delayed reaction to their father's absence; boys experience emotional upheavals earlier and get over it sooner. Girls on the other hand experience pain in adolescence and see men as a source of rescue or rejection. *But whether a child is male or female, fathers are needed for their 'otherness,' to put a healthy wedge between mother and child, to be a haven from real or imagined maternal injustice or excessive hovering* (p.7).

Playing the dual role of Mother and Father
According to Secunda, mothers and fathers are important because they are models of feminity/ masculinity to their daughters/sons, and are examples of how one reacts to the other. Children learn about men and women, not only by being with each parent but also by observing their parents' relationship. It is from both parents that children gain their basic identity.

Emphasizing the importance of Father-daughter relationships, Secunda opined:

If a daughter is unable to win her father's approval for herself, and not simply her achievements or "womanly" virtues, she may believe that she is unacceptable to other men, or she may choose men who can never measure up to her image of Daddy. She may believe that she can't live without a man – or that all men are no damn good. So what are fathers for? What is their unique value to girls? I believe a father can provide any or all of the following to his daughter:

One man's opinion – *a viewpoint and way of being, a source of emotional and intellectual tutelary richness that is different from Mom's.*

One man's history – *continuity from his past to her future, knowledge from his experience, his victories and failures.*

One man's chemistry – *his genes mingling with hers; his face and features, inflections and temperament, moods and instincts, all contributing to the alchemy of her personality.*

One man's empathy - *a haven from mother, a court of appeal, a source of perspective.*

One man's body – *his beard and scent, his frame and strength, his touch and sheltering arms, giving her the first, wondrous feel of a loving man's physical intimacy.*

One man's charmed attention *– a chance to rehearse, in a way that she cannot with her mother, what love with a man can be like.*

One man's validation *– a chance to voice and test her opinions, which he will not perceive as betrayals.*

One man's adaptability *– the capacity to weather with equanimity the seasons of his own life as well as hers.*

One man's willingness to learn *– from the triumphs and tragedies of her life, as well as his own. Without any of that a daughter aches with questions. She has no dress rehearsals for heterosexual friendship and love – a handicap from which many women, their emotional histories littered with shattered hopes, never recover. Without a father's dependable involvement a woman is in some way forever incomplete, and "men" are so much theory (pp. 28, 29).*

Secunda further stated that a mother can make up for many things but she cannot replace a father, especially when it comes to how her daughter feels about herself in her intimate connections with men.

The same would hold true for a father's relationship with his son. Both parents are important, not only in terms of modeling male-female relationship, but also in relation to one's sexual identity. Sexual identity is shaped by the parent, hence the need for appropriate role models, especially in the early stages of children's development. According to Balswick & Balswick, (1999) between the ages of two to four years of age children develop a sense of sexual identity; and this issue is revisited between ages sixteen to twenty-two when revisions are made.

How a person relates to a partner is also dependent on one's early recollections of one's parents' marriage. If it was conflictual, hostile or terminated, the relationship is likely to follow a similar pattern. Since much of learning is about taking risks, being greater risk takers than mothers generally, fathers play a critical role in the academic competence and confidence of their children. By virtue of their association with their fathers, children are more confident and are more comfortable in taking risks themselves, thereby increasing their competencies and knowledge base.

Boys from homes where the father is absent tend to be less differentiated than other boys. They tend to be more dependent on others to determine behaviour and are more passive in their approach to their environment. The absence of a male role model may affect how they see themselves and how they relate to the opposite sex. They are likely to adopt the role of the mother and, in so doing have difficulty in achieving masculine identity.

Too, the mother-son relationship can become so enmeshed that the son's dependence on his mother extends beyond adolescence. As a result, the son may fail to develop satisfactory relationships or achieve independence even in manhood. In instances where he manages to achieve a certain level of independence and is married, the mother may dog his footsteps, and to his wife becomes the meddling mother-in-law. If the son is not strong enough, she may be a source of discord between him and his wife, thereby causing a strain on the marriage or severance of the marital relationship.

Some parents project their instability onto their children by seeking assurance and stability from them. Through projection parents transmit their lack of differentiation to the children and by so doing cause them to resonate their instability or psychosis.

For these and other reasons, children of divorced homes tend to do poorly socially, academically and physically and are more likely to experience a divorce themselves. It is also believed that children of divorced parents have a low commitment to marriage and the tendency to marry at an early age – which is a factor for an unstable marriage (ibid).

Conditions under which divorce is less troubling

Balswick & Balswick (1999, pp. 313, 314) suggested the following conditions under which the psychosocial effects of divorce are least troubling:

1. *When parents discuss the possibility of a divorce beforehand and continue to discuss the situation after it has occurred.*
2. *Where there is less hostility between parents.*
3. *When parents maintain an affable relationship with each other and continue to show love and respect for the children.*
4. *When the parent who has custody stresses obedience, respect, good behaviour and affection.*
5. *When the parent who was not awarded custody spends time with the children.*
6. *When the parents' post-divorce communication is good.*
7. *When parents have a good relationship, joint custody works well, and children exhibit a greater self-esteem.*
8. *When custody is split, custody by a parent of the same sex seems to be most beneficial. However, sibling separation may hurt rather than help the adjustment process.*

But how about divorcee-parents? How might they cope with separation?

6

Coping with Separation

People involved in a dysfunctional marriage ought to seek the help of a professional counselor. Marriage partners may be pleasantly surprised that differences can be amicably worked out – that the marriage may be revived and renewed with professional help; but the couple needs to seek help early. The sooner professional help is obtained the more the likelihood of the problems being resolved. Through counseling, couples can learn problem-solving skills and attain a greater understanding and clarification of issues they are facing.

Counseling will not solve every marital problem or prevent people from divorcing, but it increases the likelihood of a successful marriage and mitigates the effects of a divorce. Divorce is not something that should be taken lightly, for divorce does not necessarily solve marital problems. This is proven by the fact that many divorced couples bring the same problems into new relationships. It is therefore crucial that the issues impacting the marriage be attended to patiently, prayerfully, spiritually or biblically and practically.

Notwithstanding, at times divorce is inevitable and sometimes desirable. If divorce is inevitable or desirable, find a good Christian attorney – one who has the spiritual depth and acumen to handle the matter while allowing you to keep your dignity intact. Many lawyers are often too adversarial in their approach and consequently give bad advice. A person should not surrender one's principles on the altar of expediency. Remember, long after the case is settled you will have to deal with the consequences of actions taken. Therefore, seek a win-win settlement. In some cases an aggressive analytic lawyer is needed, but such instances are rare. Nonetheless, be prepared to deal with reactions for every action.

In order to avoid costly court battles, it is best to seek an out-of-court settlement. Don't waste time in protracted court battles. They may drain you physically, emotionally, financially and spiritually. Settle quickly and move on. Bear in mind that there is wisdom in peace. One can win only to lose. Or one can lose only to win.

A divorced person may need help in working through issues such as feelings of rejection, abandonment, betrayal, low self-esteem, guilt, regret, depression, single parenting, co-parenting arrangements, lifestyle change, identity issues, economic adjustments, security issues and living arrangements – essentially the need to make psychological and structural adjustments.

A small group of trusted friends committed to praying with divorcees about issues and with whom divorcees can share freely may be helpful. Friendship or companionship with other people is crucial to healing; but it will take a skilled counselor to journey with divorcees, to hold divorcees together, to prevent a divorcee from behaving irrationally or vindictively toward the ex-spouse.

One of the worse things divorcees can do is to panic. This will cause an immense set back. I find the following extracted from Landers (1996) to be helpful:

Golden Rules for Coping with Panic
1. Remember that although your feelings and symptoms are frightening, they are neither dangerous nor harmful.

2. Understand that what you are experiencing is merely an exaggeration of your normal reactions to stress.
3. Do not fight your feelings or try to wish them away. The more willing you are to face them, the less intense they will become.
4. Don't add to your panic by thinking about what "might happen." If you find yourself asking, "What if?" tell yourself, "So what!"
5. Stay in the present. Be aware of what is happening to you rather than concern yourself with how much worse it might get.
6. Label your fear level from zero to 10 and watch it go up and down. Notice that it doesn't stay at a very high level for more than a few seconds.
7. When you find yourself thinking about fear, change your "what if?" thinking. Focus on and perform some simple, manageable tasks. Notice that when you stop thinking frightening thoughts your anxiety fades.
8. When fear comes, accept it, don't fight it. Wait, and give it time to pass. Don't try to escape from it. Be proud of the progress you've made. Think about how good you will feel when the anxiety has passed and you are in total control and at peace.

Be positive. One's outlook on life will determine one's outcome. Granted, it is difficult to be positive when experiencing feelings of defeat, disappointment, guilt, shame, pain, grief, and anger, and so on. Nevertheless, one needs to ask one self, what is the alternative? When all is said and done, it is reliance upon one's inner resources and direct dependence upon God that will enable a person to go through life's trials successfully.

Divorcees may draw on spiritual resources and upon God-given abilities in the most trying of circumstances. Defeat and failure are never final. As long as there is life, there is hope. Each person has the capacity to talk one's self out of negative emotions and embrace failure as just another experience gained in the "University of Hard Knocks." We learn, and we move on. Divorcees can develop inner fortitude and can mature much faster on account of life's apparent failures.

The task of single parenting and the task of taking care of personal needs at the same time will prove to be formidable challenges. Yet, divorced persons have the assurance that "God never allows more than we can bear." This may sound simplistic but it is simply profound. God is able to help divorcees go through all the difficulties that accompany divorce.

A major difficulty accompanying divorce is that of accepting the divorce. Some divorcees will require a longer time before they are able to accept divorce is now a part of their experience. The sooner the divorce is accepted, however, the sooner the divorced person will be able to move on in life. Refusal to accept divorce will prolong the grief.

Some divorcees tend to exaggerate the experience or to feel that their experience is unique. But experiences are never unique, and one is never alone. Many people have been there, while others are currently going through similar experiences. Unfortunately, that's life.

While trying to come to terms with the divorce, some people may suffer from low self-esteem and lose their confidence. Dealing with low self-esteem and the corresponding loss of confidence are difficult hurdles to overcome. The key is self-acceptance – accepting yourself as you are – and not what you wish to be – and without comparison to anyone.

Divorcees can love and accept self because everyone is loved unconditionally by the Creator of the universe, is accepted by Him, and is therefore worthy of esteem. Divorced people are valued and valuable because as human beings they bear the image of God. God has demonstrated how much He values people and the extent of His love by sending His one and only Son to die for everyone (John 3:16).

In John 4, the Bible provides a good example of a divorced woman whom Jesus deliberately sought after and helped. Apparently, the woman, a Samaritan, suffered from low self-esteem and so deliberately went to draw water at a time of day when no one was expected to be at the well. But Jesus joined himself to her and engaged the woman in conversation. At the time, most Jews would have regarded the woman as a "nobody" because of her moral failures and because she was from a "mongrel" tribe.

Since she was a divorced woman and the product of an inter-racial marriage, the woman faced double jeopardy in society. Her five failed marriages did not augur well for her; plus she was living with a man that was not her husband, and she was a Samaritan. "The Jews had no dealings with the Samaritans" (John 4:9). In spite of all this, Jesus accepted the woman who formally retreated from society. By showing the woman love and compassion, the woman apparently experienced moral and spiritual healing and was reintegrated in society. It is a fact that God loves and accepts unconditionally everyone, including people who are divorced.

God is the most qualified person to inform the value we put on self and how we feel towards self. Instead of turning on self in self-loathing and guilt, divorcees can accept God's view of self and see themselves as people of worth. Many divorcees need to learn how to love self. On the road to recovery, loving God and loving self are primary steps divorcees need to take.

Loving self includes loving your body, and so caring for it. Apart from its physical benefits, physical exercise can be very useful in dealing with issues of self-esteem and in dealing with depression. Divorcees should therefore make exercise a part of their daily routine. Participating in something divorcees enjoy such as dancing, walking, aerobics, karate, football, cricket, tennis, squash, and so on are great in alleviating stress. Before embarking on any serious physical exercise, however, divorcees would need to see a medical doctor. The doctor will give a thorough physical exam and advise on the nature of the exercise you should pursue.

Another crucial recovery strategy is involvement in a church or service club, or simply helping someone else in need on a consistent basis. Such activities can be quite therapeutic. Divorcees will find that by paying attention to the needs of others, divorcees will begin to feel better about self and will have less time to worry about personal problems.

Another strategy relates to the pervasive problem of guilt. The following was submitted by an anonymous person to psychologist and family counselor, Dr. James Dobson:

When my wife left me for another man, I felt like the whole thing was my fault. I still feel that way. I had never even looked at another woman, yet here I am taking the blame for her affair. Rationally, I know I am being very unfair to myself, but I can't help it. Or can I? Dr. Dobson responded with words of wisdom:

> *You must resist the temptation to take all the blame. I'm not recommending that you sit around hating your wife. Bitterness and resentment are emotional cancers that rot us from within. However, I would encourage you to examine the facts carefully. Ask yourself these questions: Despite my many mistakes and failures in my marriage, did I value my family and try to preserve it? Did my wife decide to destroy it and then seek justification for her actions? Was I given a fair chance to resolve the areas of greatest irritation? Could I have held her even if I had made all the changes she wanted? Is it reasonable that I should hate myself for this thing that has happened?*
>
> *If you examine objectively what has occurred, you might begin to see yourself as a victim of your wife's irresponsibility rather than a worthless failure at the game of love (Dobson, 1997, pp. 452, 453).*

Another problem divorcees may have to face is that of dealing with a vindictive ex-spouse. The temptation is to respond in kind, but that will only add fuel to the fire. Do not underestimate the power of prayer to deal with this admittedly difficult problem.

If you are already involved in another relationship before the divorce is finalized, or shortly thereafter, be good enough not to flaunt the new relationship before your ex-spouse. Be sensitive to the feelings of your ex-partner. Remember that your ex may be smarting from the separation. Acts of reprisals may become the norm. Some persons ego cannot stand the thought of their ex being with somebody else (at least not so soon), and may attempt to make one's life miserable.

Security wise, it is important divorcees not take anything for granted. One never truly knows with whom one is dealing until a person feels hurt or is upset. Love and hate are powerful emotions – they can both lead to fits of madness or strange uncharacteristic behaviour.

Children in divorce situations are casualties. Careful and sympathetic planning, plus constructive and constant supervision will be necessary. Adequate preparation should be made for their care, whether nursery, home care, or after school. The parent having custody should encourage the children to talk about what is happening at school, day care, etc. so that they can get a feel of how they are coping. Caregivers may be alerted to note changes in behaviour patterns.

In providing for the emotional needs of children, parents should share important information regarding the children's health, welfare and general interests. However, each parent should develop independent relationships with teachers, doctors, coaches and friends in order not to rely on the other parent for information. Taking turns to accompany the children on field trips, to the doctor, or dentist and others will be helpful. This will give the children a greater sense of security. By simply sending a copy of the children's school report to the non-custodial parent helps in improving the relationship between parents. It also gives the children a sense that both parents are interested in their welfare or that they are not abandoned by one of them.

As a parent, it is inappropriate to pretend that you are not experiencing sad feelings, (if they do exist) and to prevent the children from acknowledging and expressing their own feelings. Admit to your feelings. This not only help you in terms of dealing with your own feelings but it also helps the children to acknowledge their own. Studies show that 30% to 50% of children from divorced families suffer from depression (Hendricks, 1990). Therefore children should be made to know that it is okay to feel sad. It is vital for them to be allowed to mourn the loss of a family member or express their anger at whomsoever they perceived caused the divorce. This is the first step toward emotional healing.

Being honest with oneself and the situation is a major step toward the solution. A parent may show the children what they can do and encourage them to give God those circumstances that they cannot change. Children may also be encouraged to be involved in constructive activities. Being constructively busy minimizes the effects of dejection.

Look on the positive side. The separation provides an opportunity for a parent to gently guide children in problem solving techniques as well as an opportunity for parents to model the required behaviour. It is not enough to tell a child that God cares and will provide; parents must truly demonstrate belief.

Also, children do not need to know the details of the divorce. This invariably triggers contempt. One should guard against resentment and spite for the absent parent. It is wise to refrain from derogatory remarks about the ex-spouse. This does further damage to the children. Acceptance and assurance of love are critical factors. Children need to have the love of both parents (even though they might not be living under the same roof). This is very important, and this reality must be demonstrated, affirmed, and reinforced.

Divorce does not break the parent-child bond. Though the ex-wife or ex-husband may no longer live at home, the children can still benefit from having a warm relationship with her/him. The problem is that the parent having custody may feel angry toward the ex-partner and resent any involvement with the children. Hence, the custody parent bashes the ex-partner in front of the children and uses ingenuous ways to prevent or discourage the children from spending time with the ex-spouse. But that is not good. Care must be taken that anger does not lead to spiteful actions.

Oates (1997) identified the following as detrimental to children's stability:

> *First, the degree of civility between the parents in the divorce process makes the transition more bearable for children. The presence of uncontrolled rage, character assassination, or brutality in physical violence destabilizes children. Second, the peaceful access of the children to both parents after the divorce makes stability more certain. Third, stability is increased if the children are faithfully supported financially by both parents. Divorce can dissolve a marriage but should not destabilize the children; they are the one flesh personified. Fourth, grandparents can be either a negative or positive factor (p. 37).*

Assuming that the demise of the marriage is clearly one parent's fault, helping the children to put the shortcomings of the estranged parent in perspective is a healthier approach than bashing the ex-spouse. Children need to come to terms with the fact that their parents are fallible, imperfect human-beings who should be loved and respected nonetheless.

The well-being of children must be a primary concern. *Children's well-being is inversely correlated with the level of post-divorce conflicts that exists and persists between parents* (Rice, 2001). Being angry is understandable at times, but to be controlled by anger is wrong and can be dangerous.

Ask yourself: Can a child learn to trust a man or woman if the child is constantly told how 'bad' the father or mother is? Can a boy develop a stable, manly personality if he is constantly told: *You are just like your father*? Or, can a girl develop a stable feminine personality if she is constantly told: *You are just like your mother*? Can children have a healthy view of authority if they are taught to despise their father/mother or are not made to see them regularly?

If this wrong attitude of undermining the children's relationship with a parent is to be corrected, forgiving the ex-spouse is crucial. In this regard, especially for Christians, praying sincerely for an ex-spouse is important. There is perhaps no better approach than this. Bashing the ex-partner is definitely bad. Prayer, however, makes it difficult to bash the person you have been praying for. Avoid dwelling on the past, lest you be filled with anger and regrets. One cannot change the past. But you can chart the future, to a great extent. Obsession with the future, however, may cause you to live in fear and may rob you of the blessing of the moment. In regard to your attitude and actions, make the right choices today, and tomorrow will take care of it's self.

In spite of your good intentions and great efforts, however, the wind of misfortune may assail you. Purveyors of evil may attempt to block your progress and might even try to destroy you. Circumstances of life may rock your boat again and again. But have faith in God and trust Him to carry you through. He will.

I find Mallicoat's poem to be quite uplifting. She says:

> *I was regretting the past and fearing the future.*
> *Suddenly my Lord was speaking:*
> *"My name is **I AM**."*
>
> *He paused. I waited. He continued.*
> *"When you live in the past with its mistakes and regrets,*
> *It is hard. I am not there.*
> *My name is not **I WAS**."*

"When you live in the future, with its problems and fears,
It is hard. I am not there.
*My name is not **I WILL BE.**"*

"When you live in this moment,
It is not hard. I am here.
*My name is **I AM.**"*

- Helen Mallicoat

Divorcees need to guard against becoming so distraught because of an ex's weakness that divorcees become virtually obsessed with thoughts of the ex-spouse. Such an attitude results in maintaining a psychological connection long after the divorce, thus hampering one's ability to move on. Divorcees lose power when they allow the ex-partner to pull their strings from a distance. As long as a person dwells unduly on what other people have done "to them," one will never experience the freedom to move on nor the liberty and empowerment to take charge of one's future.

Playing the role of victim may lead to feelings of anger, bitterness, and resentment, which do more harm to the person so possessed than the object of that person's anger. Negative emotions poison one's immune system thereby affecting a person's wellbeing, not only emotionally, but also physically. One's interpersonal relationships are impacted negatively as well.

It is important also that divorcees do not unnecessarily involve children in disputes. When the need to express frustration occurs, divorcees should share it with someone other than the children, namely a trusted friend or counselor? A distinct danger is for the parent who has custody of the children to over relate to a child. In so doing the parent inadvertently make a substitute mate out of the child, thereby adding to the stress the child faces.

Children cannot withstand the emotional overload of distraught parents. Accordingly Hendricks (1990, p. 142) admonished: "Don't treat the child like a parent. Too much responsibility can hurt the child. Don't use the child as messenger. If the child feels torn between loyalties, he will feel guilty if he does not take sides. Don't let the child manipulate. Both parents need to discipline the child and teach him/her responsibility."

The above are excellent principles which ought to be followed diligently. Boundaries between parents and children should not become blurred. If a son is expected to be "the man of the house" he will feel overburdened. By having to serve as a mother's confidante, a daughter too can become overwhelmed. Children need to be assured that parents will take care of them, not vice versa. Even though their family situation is not ideal, responsible parenting can make children feel more secure.

In divorce situations, the behaviour of children needs to be carefully noted and monitored. Disturbed social adjustment, eating and sleeping disorders are not uncommon. Aggressive behaviours, illnesses (real or imagined) may multiply and lack of self-esteem may grow. A child may revert to infantile behaviour as a way of expressing disapproval over the divorce. Some children may show extreme apathy and others may become hyperactive. But this too will pass. Love, a firm hand, and a "cool head" are required.

It is the responsibility of parents to provide a stable and predictable environment. This fact cannot be overstated. Accordingly, divorcees need to be particularly watchful when there is frequent moving and disruption in income, sickness or tragedy in the family. These events may threaten the children's upward mobility (educationally and otherwise), not to mention feelings of insecurity.

One area of a child's life most likely to be affected is school performance. The child is likely to become fearful and worried and may be unable to concentrate on school work. Each child needs to be assured that he/she will make it; when failure occurs it should be accepted, and the child encouraged to keep on trying. Although a parent cannot make it all right, words of love and concern can help. A parent must show sympathy.

Divorcee-parents may also encourage their children to relate with well-adjusted children of other divorced parents. This may give divorcee-children a sense that they are not alone in their situation, and may provide an outlet to share feelings and experiences without fear. This forum may also be helpful in terms of passing on coping skills to each other.

Ignoring the concerns of children in divorce situations can be consequential, even devastating. Unfortunately, sometimes divorcee-parents are so absorbed in their lives and careers that they provoke feelings of alienation and rejection in their children. As a result, some children attempt suicide. A young person who cannot adequately equate values may very well decide that the best way out of being "poor," for example, is to hurt oneself.

To avoid tragedy in the life of children parents need to be in touch with their children and to develop an awareness or sensitivity in relating to them. This will help to identify needs and alleviate deep emotional feelings. When children feel needed and appreciated at home they are less likely to "want out" of life.

Both parents need to be involved in helping to maintain some semblance of normalcy and predictability in children's lives. Helping children to cope is too big a job for one individual. Other people such as school teachers, church workers, and other responsible role models may also be co-opted as part of a support group for children. Opportunities for divorcee-children to engage in part-time jobs, volunteer work, or to participate activities which develop responsibility and thereby a sense of achievement should be sought, made available and encouraged. This level of involvement helps to keep a person going.

It is important to maintain one's support networks and to take advantage of them when necessary. Understanding familiar faces, and being in regular places have therapeutic potential. Such faces and places provide a safe haven or refuge when the need arises. "Safe" people and places are constants in the equation of things, helping to solve problems, or, at the least, providing the bases to figure things out. Parents should therefore not make any major life changes such as relocating, changing of job, or remarrying just yet. Apart from the fact that judgment may somewhat be impaired at this time, stability and emotional support are critical at this juncture.

Also, divorcees should not dwell on "why" questions. Knowing why is important, but divorcees can spend a lifetime asking why and still not find the answers. Furthermore, much of the 'answers' divorcees will receive or arrive at on their own will be speculative. For now, divorcees should accept the fact that they are creatures with a free will and that even in the most perfect environment, like Adam and Eve people may yield to temptation or make choices inimical to their best interest. Dealing with the situation as it presents itself and what needs to be done is more likely to lead to speedier acceptance and recovery than asking why.

Yet it is not unusual for a divorced person to move from asking why things are the way they are to question why these things happen **to me**. The danger with that is that if a person gets stuck in the "Why me?" mode, he/she makes self a victim, and hence generally fail to accept responsibility for choices made, and may blame others or circumstances instead. Failure to accept responsibility for personal contribution to the situation not only prolongs the pain, but divorcees may get caught in a psychological paralysis, resulting in depression. Divorcees may become extremely transfixed into feeling sorry for self (hence the pity party), and in feelings of anger toward the ex-spouse. As a result, divorcees may take on the appearance of a masochist or manifest a martyr complex.

Life is like a puzzle. But divorcees need not give up when the pieces do not quite fi t together. With perseverance, training and faith in God everyone may eventually succeed in figuring things out. And there is nothing to be ashamed of if the divorce was based on Scriptural grounds. In fact, divorcees may need to acknowledge their strength and affirm self for having taken appropriate action, instead of committing "marrydumb."

If the divorce was clearly the fault of one person, the guilty party should be encouraged to seek God's forgiveness and the forgiveness of the ex-spouse. Forgiveness of self is also in order. Divorcees should carefully evaluate the experience, learn form it, and move on with life. There is no point in mortifying self over the past. People of strength do fall down at times, but they do get up afterwards. If the divorce was sinful, divorcees do not have to pay penance, because the blood of Jesus cleanses from **all sin**.

Divorcees can also draw strength from the experience of David and others in the Bible who successfully overcame failure. Divorcees may find it instructive to note that a divorce is not the end of the road; albeit, an unfortunate part of divorcees' journey. Divorcees can rebound – become much wiser and stronger – love more maturely and live more fully. Divorcees can come through divorce better than they were before, as mistakes and failures can indeed be turned into learning experiences. Divorcees need to have hope and faith that things will get better after a while.

After a While

After a while, you learn the subtle difference
Between holding a hand and chaining a soul,
And you learn that love doesn't mean leaning
And company doesn't mean security,
And you begin to learn that kisses aren't contracts
And presents aren't promises,
And you begin to accept your defeats
With your head up and your eyes open
With the grace of a woman (or man), not the grief of a child
And you learn to build all your roads on today
Because tomorrow's ground is too uncertain for plans.

And futures have a way of falling down in mid-flight.
After a while, you learn
That even sunshine burns if you get too much.
So you plant your own garden and decorate your own soul,
Instead of waiting for someone to bring you flowers.
And you learn that you really can endure.
That you really are strong.
And you really do have worth.
And you learn and learn.
With every goodbye you learn.

- Veronica A. Shoffstall

7

Coping with Relationship Baggage

Some people believe that the best way to get over a past relationship is to start a new one. But just a word of caution here: divorcees need to be careful that they do not "jump out of the frying pan into the fire." Divorcees need to give space to rebuild fences and to deal appropriately with "baggage." There is usually a lot of baggage to be sorted and disposed of during the healing process.

It is important that healing takes place before thoughts of another relationship is entertained. Healing allows for better judgment and the increased likelihood of successful interpersonal relationships. Although remarriage may be desirable by some divorcees, they are well advised to recognize that remarriage is not an easy transition, especially where children are involved.

The couple should take some time, not just to plan the wedding, but also to plan their future as one family. As such, divorced persons need to approach remarriage prayerfully, perceptively, biblically or spiritually and practically. In the final analysis, parents need to be at a certain level of maturity; they need to have patience; they need to have a heart of sincere love; and faith in God to work things out.

Merging families have issues of their own. Bevcar and Bevcar (2003) noted that in order to achieve stepchildren integration, the following tasks are necessary:

- Mourning the losses involved
- Development of new traditions
- Formation of new interpersonal relationships
- Maintenance of relationship(s) with child(ren)'s biological parents
- Satisfactory movement between households

There are indeed many challenges involved in merging families. The formation of a new identity is the overriding issue. Children and parents are immersed in a milieu of the unfamiliar – an unfamiliar place in many instances, an unfamiliar culture, unfamiliar faces with their own nuances. Coming from a context of divorce and single parenting make the adjustment all the more challenging.

Other challenges include (1) the issue of relating to a new husband or wife; (2) the issue of parenting stepchildren; (3) the issue of managing or blending the family as a new and cohesive unit; (4) the issue of relating to stepbrothers or sisters; (5) the issue of relating to stepparents.

Parents as well as children will experience challenges in the "step" relationships. Parents who have never had children of their own are particularly affected. The lack of experience in raising children of their own, and the lack of proper parental models in their homes as children may make the stepparent relationship of the remarried even more challenging. In this regard, Reed (1992, pp. 106-110) has made some useful suggestions for stepmothers and stepfathers.

Guidelines for stepmothers:
- Understand your role as a stepmother
- Accept the reality of the former spouse

- Be gentle with yourself and all family members
- Seek fulfillment in several areas of life

Guidelines for stepfathers:
- Give the new relationships time to develop
- Take an active part in establishing household rules and values
- Encourage the children to spend time with their mother without you
- Be clear about your needs and desires for the family and the relationships

Stepparents may experience resentment from their own children for sharing love, time, and attention with stepsiblings. As a result, stepparents will need to take time to discuss children's fears and expectations. Stepparents may experience resentment from step children. Stepchildren may be hypercritical and accusatory. They may perceive or imagine excuses for resenting the stepparent. The stepparent may be resented for:

- Breaking up their home (whether it is true or not)
- Keeping dad/mom from remarrying their mom/dad (whether true or not)
- For being too young/old
- Doing things differently
- Making dad/mom happy
- Sharing dad's/mom's time

Submitting to discipline by stepparents may be a problem for some children. Children may resent the stepparent if children are of the opinion that the stepparent was responsible for the breakup of the previous marriage. In addition, there could be increased hostility if children perceive the stepparent to be attempting to replace the biological noncustodial parent. All of this could make discipline virtually impossible and severely impact the new marriage. Children function better when there is an obvious acknowledgement and respect for their biological parents. Irrespective of the level of the non-custodial parents' involvement in children's lives, they generally do not wish for their biological parents to be replaced. Children desire to maintain their blood ties.

Bevcar and Bevcar (2003) also noted additional complications. These included: family members with different loyalties and different amounts of previously shared history; lack of an adjustment period without children; increased sexual tensions rising out of the newly formed husband-wife relationship, as well as the lack of incest taboos between stepparents and stepchildren. Bevcar and Bevcar further pointed out that: "It is a myth to think that all members will automatically become a single-family unit similar to the one experienced in previous families. Indeed, the new family can never hope to be just like the old one" (p.120).

Reed (1992) noted that children of a blended family may experience low self-esteem if they see themselves as different from children of homes where both biological parents are present. In the eyes of divorcee-children, the blended family is not as "real."

Emotional needs factor highly in all families, more so in families affected by divorce. There are three basic emotional needs common to everyone. These are: the need to feel loved and have a sense of belonging; the need to feel acceptable and have a sense of worthiness; the need to feel adequate and have a sense of competence (Kincaid, 1996). Where these needs are unfulfilled, family members, including children, may suffer from low self-esteem. Reed (1992) averred parents can help children to build positive self-esteem in the following ways: (1) give credit for accomplishment; (2) communicate confidence in children; and (3) let them know you value them.

Although stepparents need to accept and take the role of parenting seriously, stepparents need to understand that they can never replace the biological parent. As such, stepparents should be realistic about expectations. They should not fight the influence nor compete with the biological parent; instead biological parents should be allowed to play an active role in children's lives.

Also, stepparents need to guard against accepting blame for everything that goes wrong in the home; and should accept problems as challenges. The successful resolution of challenges increases bonding. In addition, stepparents should have varied interests and seek satisfaction from sources other than the family.

Advisedly, if the challenges the family faces as a result of remarriage are to be overcome, it is important to start on the right footing. Careful and prayerful selection of a partner before marrying into a family is in order, plus premarital counseling. A person needs to approach remarriage with as much as possible stacked in favour of the marriage succeeding.

8

Care for a Troubled Relationship

In this chapter, a model for pastoral intervention and care will be presented. The model focuses on counselors' spiritual and professional preparation to meet counselees' needs. The need of the counselee is integral to the process; it is the basis on which counseling strategies are formulated and decisions made. In this regard, the counselor needs to be discerning and spiritually wise. He/She should be knowledgeable about marriage and the possible causes of divorce and remarriage.

Pastoral counselors' involvement with clients invariably includes a theological understanding of what constitutes a marriage, and the scriptural bases for divorce and remarriage. Such involvement also includes an appreciation for some of the possible causes for divorce, an understanding of the psychosocial effects of divorce and remarriage – how divorce and remarriage affect the family system, and how each family member may be affected. Counselors should also be aware of good ethical principles and be knowledgeable of counseling issues. In addition, counselors should be in a position to suggest strategies for coping with divorce and should have the ability to prepare clients for remarriage and the conjoint family.

Yet the counselors' preparation is only one side of the coin. Couples' approach to marital difficulties and to counseling itself is just as crucial. There are two basic approaches couples take to marital difficulties.

When overwhelmed by problems, they determine either to fight or to take a flight. If the marriage is worth fighting for, some will fight for it; if not, they will flee. Yet fighting for one's marriage or fleeing from it is not so simple. For there are some couples who do not know how to fight for their family – some lack the skill – others lack the will; and some are fighting for a marriage that for all practical purposes no longer exists.

In any case couples experiencing marital difficulties ought to seek the help of a professional counselor as soon as possible. A person may be pleasantly surprised that differences can be amicably worked out, one's marriage revived and renewed through professional help. The reality is that there is no marriage that is trouble free. Anywhere you have two human beings sharing the same space for a considerable period of time you are bound to have problems.

Often what makes one marriage successful and another unsuccessful is how problems are managed. Notwithstanding, couples facing difficulties in their marriage invariably entertain thoughts of divorce. To divorce or not to divorce, that is the question. For some, divorce is the easy way out.

COUNSELLING ISSUES
As it is important for one to be clear as to what constitutes a marriage and the need to work at building the relationship, it is important to be clear as to why a person of a troubled marriage may be seeking the services of a pastoral counselor.

Need for clarity
Firstly, there is the need for clarity. Accordingly, the counselor needs to know the nature of the problem – what it is that the counselee is facing or having to deal with; and specifically what is happening in the relationship that is causing the

disharmony. The goal of the counselor at this point is not just to gather information but to also put the client's problem in perspective.

Information provided by the counselee will form the basis of the counselor's assessment, and to determine the direction in which the counseling goes. In light of this the counselor needs to test for accuracy and probe for additional information to assist the counseling process. In process, if new information is provided which conflict the information previously received or which enhances the counselor's knowledge of the counselee's problem/s, the counselor should be wise enough and tactful enough to steer the counseling in a new direction, if necessary.

In gathering information, the counselor needs to be aware that the presenting problem is often not the real issue, and as such he/she may have to peel away at layers of side issues before getting to the heart of the matter. The counselor should bear in mind also that clients sometimes deliberately withhold information until they have tested the counselor's competency, feel comfortable with the counselor before they bare their souls, or feel confident enough to divulge sensitive information about themselves. In addition, some situations are extremely exaggerated in the heat of the moment, and the client may begin to panic. The counselor's job is to restore calm and to help the client have a balanced perspective. These scenarios require much patience and tolerance.

Where it is alleged that one party has done something to undermine the marriage or has repeatedly done so, it may be helpful for the client to give a history of the problem. That is – say when the problem actually started – when it is likely to occur – and the frequency of its occurrence. Some problems may be related to acts of provocation or insensitivity, depression or trauma caused by the loss of a loved one or loss of job, hormone imbalance, the seasons of life such as midlife crisis, a time of financial stress or insecurity, sickness or any major life-changing event. Connecting the problem to a particular event or incident, a significant period of life, and so on may provide additional insights into the problem, provide helpful clues as to its source or may put a different face on the problem altogether.

In addition, a family history may be helpful to ascertain any ecological link with the existing problem or any problems that might have been handed down from previous generations. For example, an alcoholic person may discover that the abuse of alcohol is a part of their family history and so treating it may demand extra effort to break the chain.

It is also imperative to get a sense of how the couple has handled problems in the past and what efforts have been made to deal with the present situation. Efforts at reconciling their differences, or the lack thereof, will provide useful information as to the couple's level of commitment to each other, including their problem-solving skills.

The counselor also needs to know how the counselee is being affected by his/her context. Accordingly, a thorough physical exam is in order, a psychological evaluation and spiritual assessment. If children are involved, they too need to be assessed and counseled.

In addition, as clients seek pastoral-care for various reasons, it must be abundantly clear from the very outset, as to the clients' reason/s for seeking therapeutic intervention. Is it to find help in restoring the marriage? Is it to obtain help in order to deal with the consequences of a decision that has already been made? Whatever the reason, one needs to be clear about it. In being clear about it, we must then ascertain how best to help the client.

Determine counseling strategies
In determining how best to help a client, the counselor needs to answer certain questions for him/herself. Some of these questions include:

1. Are the parties committed to each other and to making the marriage work?

2. Is the offending party (if any) repentant and amenable to change?
3. What attitude/s, if any, needs to be changed in order to create harmony?
4. What faulty beliefs and misunderstandings need to be corrected, if any?
5. What behaviour/s needs to change?

Also, it may be detrimental to the process initially for the counselor to help the client in terms of getting him/her to postpone the making of any major decision, especially if anger is perceived to be an issue to be dealt with. Or, in process, the client might need to be helped in understanding that the path that is being or is about to be pursued is largely influenced by anger. Convincing a person to delay making any decision until he/she is able to think more objectively may be the first step in helping him/her toward experiencing wholeness as some people make decisions out of anger and in doing so regrettably complicate things further. So counselors may need to help clients to face the reality of their situation and the likely impact of their actions.

In helping the client to do a reality check, some of the questions a client may need to answer for him/herself include:

1. Is the problem I am facing something that I can live with?
2. Is it something that I and my spouse can obtain help with?
3. How is the behaviour impacting me, our marriage and our children?
4. What present and future effects is my decision likely to have upon:
   - My life?
   - My lifestyle?
   - Our children?
5. How do I plan to deal with these?
6. What support system/s do I have in place?

If at all possible, the counselor should seek to save the marriage. The counselee's desires, however, are absolutely important and should form an integral part of the counseling process. While the exploration of other outcomes is in order, it is the counselee who must ultimately decide whether to divorce or not to divorce. The counselor's responsibility is to exercise due diligence during the therapeutic relationship and to guide the process toward the best practical and spiritual solution without infringing on the right of the client to make his/her own decision.

Since the universe is governed by natural and spiritual laws and we exist in community governed by human laws, decisions made should be informed by these laws and be consistent with them. Hence in fulfilling God's purpose for marriage, human laws must reflect an appreciation for natural, spiritual and moral laws, which the Creator of the universe has established to govern His creation. When we ride against the tide of these laws the journey of life will be unnecessarily rough and the marital ship may sink.

NATURALLY & LEGALLY
The decision-making process should therefore reflect an appreciation for natural and human laws and issues informed accordingly. A legal marriage in most jurisdictions shows a bias toward natural laws and is in tandem with spiritual laws. Only marriage between an adult male and an adult female is allowed, and there are certain duties that the married couple is obliged to perform. Marriage is not allowed between close family members.

Thus in the consideration of a divorce it is needful to ascertain whether any natural or human law has been violated. Recognition needs also to be made of the extent to which God obligates people to embrace human laws and encourages obedience thereto. For example, among other things, we are obliged to obey the laws of the land in respect to marriage and divorce.

Most jurisdictions allow divorce on the basis of adultery. Some will give a "no fault" divorce. Others will allow a person to sue for a divorce on the basis of the marriage being irretrievably broken down. But while there may be a legal basis for divorcing a spouse, a partner need not necessarily exercise his/her legal right to sue for a divorce. There are other laws, namely spiritual laws that should inform the counseling process; the foremost being the law of love.

The law of love

Husbands are told to love their wives (Coloss. 3:19). Wives are told to love their husbands (Titus 2:4). And we are told to love one another (1 John 4:7). So to love is not just a command; it is an obligation that we cannot fully discharge (Rom. 13:8). The law of love forces us to answer the following:

- What do you do when a spouse has chosen to love no longer or in a significant way has violated the marriage vows?
- Can one love a spouse and still choose to separate from him/her?
- Can a person love oneself and not choose to protect oneself from being destroyed in a dysfunctional marriage?

When a relationship becomes destructive, it may be time to draw the line. The Bible says, "Love your enemies" (Luke 6:27), but it did not say we ought to necessarily live with them, did it? The Bible says, "Love your neighbour as yourself" (Matt. 23:39), but it did not say to love your neighbour 'more than' yourself, did it?

It is imperative that a person not have an exaggerated opinion of oneself (Rom. 12:3), but one should think of self highly enough to protect and care for him/herself, shouldn't he/she? As such, there comes a time in some relationships when self-preservation may be perfectly in order. In fact we are told that self-preservation is the most basic of human instincts.

It is the height of human folly (or sickness) to self-destruct, or knowingly and willingly allow another person to destroy you. People who allow themselves to be destroyed by a "bad" relationship invariably suffer from low self-esteem. Often, they do not think highly of themselves and do not love themselves enough. Others feel trapped in some way, are blinded by an unevaluated tradition or are deluded by religious myths.

Whatever the case might be, we should not allow the institution of marriage to become a scapegoat for evil people to perpetuate their folly. The client's first approach should be: firstly, to lovingly communicate his/her feelings; secondly, if the situation persists, the client should seek professional counseling for self and for his/her spouse. Prayer is always in order.

Ignoring or minimizing the problem will not suffice. But bear in mind that there are some persons who do not want help; and there are some whom the client does not have the skills or the ability to cope with while sharing the same space. It may therefore be time for the client to show some 'tough' love. In some cases, failure to separate from an abusive spouse could very well put the client's life in jeopardy. It may be time to let go, even temporarily, for letting go may save the client's life and the one he/she loves.

Yet some might say: *It may be time to fast and pray, because God, through prayer, changes things*! Indeed, God is able to make a bad marriage become a good one, so married partners need to prayerfully and patiently look to God for help. Yet another may respond: *Faith without works is useless* (James 2:20). That is also true. As such, couples need to purposefully, prayerfully and practically work at resolving their issues.

The law of forgiveness
Part of the practical outworking of marital issues includes forgiveness. Whatever a person may have suffered in a dysfunctional relationship, there is always room for forgiveness. Therefore, in order for their relationship to work couples need to be constantly forgiving each other's faults and failures.

It is imperative to encourage the client to forgive. Refusal to forgive will affect how the client relates to his/her spouse, may lead to bitterness and resentment, may cloud one's judgment, and in the end may do more harm to the client than the wrong suffered.

Furthermore, we are commanded to forgive – on the basis of what Christ has done for us and because we are all sinners. And since God is so gracious to us, we too should be gracious to one another. *Be ye kind one to another, tenderhearted, forgiving one another, even as God for Christ's sake hath forgiven you* (Eph. 4:32 KJV).

Understandably, forgiving someone who has badly hurt us is never an easy thing, especially when we feel betrayed. Yet we are obliged to forgive, not only for Christ's sake, or the offender's sake, but also for our own sake. For in releasing the person and in letting go the wrong, we also release ourselves to experience healing and growth. In withholding forgiveness we inadvertently nurture the pain, suffer longer and retard our growth spiritually and psychologically. Our physical well-being is also affected as bitterness and resentment may wear away our immune system, make us susceptible to various diseases or lead to psychosomatic illnesses. Forgiveness is therefore an integral part of the client's journey toward wholeness, and is very important if married couples are to live harmoniously and peacefully.

The law of peace
We are told in the Scriptures to:
- *Seek peace and pursue it* (Psa. 34:14)
- *Follow peace with all men* (Heb. 12:14)
- *Live peaceably with all men*, if at all possible (Rom. 12:18)

It follows therefore that if it is not possible to live peaceably with everyone, there are some persons from whom we must necessarily separate. (See Proverbs 21:9, 19). The pursuit of peace, we are told, is a fruit of the Spirit (Gal. 5:22) and a mark of wisdom (James 3:18).

Peace should therefore not be restricted to mean the absence of war, fights and quarrels. Sometimes we have to declare war in order to attain peace. Our warfare is not physical but spiritual. This warfare necessarily includes the pursuit of the peace of mind of the individual and the pursuit of peace between spouses. It cannot mean acceptance of the status quo or peace at any cost. In the Scriptures quoted above, we see in every instance an active verb associated with peace. We are told to seek and pursue, follow and live it. So our journey toward wholeness undoubtedly involves the pursuit of peace.

ETHICALLY & PROFESSIONALLY

The journey toward wholeness also includes dealing with ethical issues. Ethical issues include: the right to decide, transference, counter-transference, dual relationships and confidentiality.

The right to decide

It is important to note that only the client can decide when to let go or to continue to struggle with a marriage that is dysfunctional. That decision is the inalienable right of the one traveling along the path of a troubled marriage alone to make. Since the All-wise God does not violate a person's free will nor right to decide, neither should anyone seek to enforce their will upon a client.

The counselor's tasks are: to help the client toward an accurate assessment of the problem, provide and explore possible courses of action, including a biblical resolution, and to journey with the client toward wholeness. The journey may be impeded by the counselor's exercise of undue influence upon the client, the counselee's inflexibility to change, or their unwillingness to adjust to change.

Transference

Transference may also impede the counseling process. Transference is the phenomenon in which the client's feelings and actions toward a significant other are transferred to the therapist. According to Lahey (2004, p. 575): *they are feeling and acting in the same basic ways that they feel and act toward their parents, employers, and so on.* Lahey, however, believes transference may be a source of insight into the nature of the counselee's relationship with a significant other.

But it may also have a negative impact on the therapeutic relationship. For instance: if the feelings and actions toward the counselor are negative, the counselee may have a difficulty relating to the counselor and may become hostile or resistant toward him/her. On the other hand, if the feelings are altogether positive, the counselor may not be able to continue the therapeutic relationship, depending on the nature of these feelings and actions and the counselee's ability to work through them professionally. It is not unusual for clients to 'fall in love' with their counselor, and vice-versa. Counselors need to guard against such scenarios.

Counter-transference
There is also the danger of counter-transference. In this scenario, the counselor's feelings and actions are in direct response to those projected by the client, thereby responding in a similar way as he/she would toward a significant other, as in expressing love or attraction, or hate. In both cases the therapeutic relationship may become compromised as it may no longer be possible for either the counselor or the client, or both, to maintain objectivity. Gladding (2004) is of the view that both transference and counter-transference must be worked through for the counseling relationship to be reality focused and productive.

Transference and counter-transference are not uncommon, however, as the therapeutic relationship is such that the counselor and client may connect or conflict at different levels with each other. Sometimes the connection or friction is due to as simple a matter as the counselor's physical resemblance to the object of the client's affection/disaffection. However, the onus is on the counselor to maintain a professional relationship at all times.

Dual relationships

Maintaining a professional relationship also includes the avoidance of dual relationships. A dual relationship exists when the counselor is involved with a client in more than one way as in relating to a client sexually or romantically, for example. Such double roles are construed to be a conflict of interest and may result in lack of objectivity as well.

CONFIDENTIALLY

Fundamental to a professional therapeutic relationship is the client's need for confidentiality and the counselor's regard for the same. Confidentiality is the basis for trusting the counselor and for the client's openness to therapy. It cannot be underscored enough how important this is, not only as a matter of principle but also in enhancing the therapeutic relationship.

Information shared with the counselor is often of a sensitive nature, thus the counselor is under obligation to respect the client's privacy. Accordingly, if there is a need to share any information relating to a client, the counselor should first obtain the client's permission in writing. There are exceptional cases, however, in which a counselor may not withhold information regarding a client. These include: (a) when a client is a danger to self and society as in the client being suicidal or is about to commit a crime; (b) or when the client has committed a felony. Under these circumstances the counselor is obliged to do the necessary reporting and take the necessary steps to preserve the client's life and to save others from being harmed. Nonetheless, the counselor's obligation to report under these circumstances should be made clear at the very outset so there are no surprises if such situations arise.

In summary, the counselor needs to identify the problem, clarify why the client is seeking counseling, assist the client toward an honest appraisal of the situation, guide the client toward the best possible and relevant resolution of the problem, address ethical issues and help the client reconcile possible outcomes.

In postulating a model for pastoral care, this researcher is of the view that the issues of divorce and remarriage should be dealt with spiritually, prayerfully, theologically, contextually, compassionately, professionally and practically. The model of care being proposed has its roots in the example of Jesus and the Apostle Paul. Both responded spiritually, contextually, compassionately and practically to those in need. They were spiritually aware, had the ability to reflect theologically, and responded non-judgmentally and appropriately to needs.

Both Jesus and Paul were concerned about meeting the spiritual, physical and psychological needs of people in need of pastoral care. They gave a context-specific response, demonstrated compassion and offered practical and relevant advice to those in need:

> *In the hands of the socially competent helper, the use of suggestions, advice, and directions is an adjunct to the rest of the process. Suggestions, advice and directives need not always be taken literally. They can act as stimuli to get clients to come up with their own packages* (Egan 2002, p. 214).

Therefore, what is important is to recognize people's needs and to be intentional and practical in our approach in meeting those needs. Accordingly, Jesus and the Apostle Paul did not necessarily wait for care-seekers to request help, but responded to the obvious and initiated care. By the examples set by Jesus and Paul, one may conclude that pastoral care is not something you do as a professional practice *per se*, although this may be a person's main occupation; it is who you are, a care-giver. It is a natural outflow from one who is spiritually connected enough to demonstrate love for neighbor as oneself.

The issues pertaining to divorce and remarriage are not new. Unfortunately, over the years, they have become more complex as human sinfulness take on added dimensions and due to the churches recalcitrance to adjust their perceptual framework theologically. In a bid to reconcile religious tradition with reality, as early as 1520, according to Stone (1996), the famed theologian, Martin Luther, gives the following advice to a woman whose impotent husband refused to grant her a divorce or annul the marriage:

> *Then I would further counsel her, with the consent of the man (who is not really her husband, but only a dweller under the same roof with her), to have intercourse with another, say her husband's brother, but to keep this marriage secret and to ascribe the children to the so-called putative father. The question is: Is such a woman saved and in a saved state? I answer: Certainly, because in this case an error, ignorance of the man's impotence, impedes the marriage; and the tyranny of the laws permits no divorce. But the woman is free through the divine law, and cannot be compelled to remain continent. Therefore the man ought to concede her right, and give up to some-body else the wife who is his only in outward appearance.*
>
> *Moreover, if the man will not give his consent, or agree to this separation – rather than allow the woman to burn [1 Cor. 7:9] or to commit adultery – I would counsel her to contract a marriage with another and flee to a distant unknown place. What other counsel can be given to one constantly struggling with the dangers of natural emotions? ...Is not the sin of a man who wastes his wife body and life a greater sin than that of the woman who merely alienates the temporal goods of her husband?* (pp. 7, 8).

Luther's advice must be viewed in light of Roman Catholic theology, which advocates the indissolubility of marriage, but allow for its annulment under special circumstances. In light of the woman's plight, a pastoral counselor, and especially one from the Roman Catholic tradition, may be hard-pressed for solutions.

SPIRITUALLY

Care-givers spiritual preparation is critical in determining the trajectory of the counseling process and in meeting counselees' needs. Counselors therefore need to be attuned with God. Attunement with God prepares the heart of counselors to serve humbly and non-judgmentally, helps counselors to discern the real issues, helps to focus attention on them and helps with wisdom to work through issues with counselees. Attunement with God is derived through prayer and meditation, knowledge of the Word and the leading of the Holy Spirit.

According to Stone, a correlation between pastoral care and theology necessarily include spiritual direction. He stated:

> *If the correlation of theology and pastoral care is our purpose, then spiritual direction must be our concern. It is an important bridge between theology and care. It focuses on our relationship with God – that factor in human experience from which we draw meaning, the courage to be, and the power to live an authentic life. ...Spiritual direction reminds us that a relationship with God is the overarching concern that focuses all others (while not negating or replacing them), that helps us rise beyond our basic human needs and wants to follow the Spirit's leading. In fact, spiritual direction is one method by which what is discussed in theology classes or read in theological discourses can have a direct impact on the ministry we offer. It is a place where doctrine such as sin, finitude, forgiveness, and grace can be discussed and experienced* (pp. 79, 80).

It is important then to include God into the picture and to invite His help every step of the way.

PRAYERFULLY

Pastoral care-giving necessarily involves God in the counseling process. There needs to be reliance upon Him for spiritual discernment and for wisdom to apprehend the situation –

for God's direction and guidance throughout the process – not to mention the need for the comforting presence of the Holy Spirit (the Counselor) to heal the wound of the hurting. This necessitates prayer and a submissive mind to the leading or guidance of the Spirit.

There are some cases that appear so hopeless on the natural level, it seems the only reasonable thing to do is to close the chapter on the relationship; but through prayer God can change that. The temptation sometimes is to accept things at face-value, concede defeat and take the easy way out of a troubled marriage, especially where suffering is involved.

Suffering though is not necessarily an indication as to the direction a person should go; that is, whether a person should seek a divorce or not on account of personal suffering. Suffering underscores the need for prayer – to invite God's healing and wisdom in the matter. Moreover, some suffering is a result of growth, misunderstandings, faulty assumptions, ignorance and a host of other things which may be corrected with the help of a skilled counselor, over time.

Stivers and others (1994) explained:

> *The degree of suffering involved is not, in itself, an indication of the appropriateness of divorce. A physician would not help a patient with appendicitis to die merely because her immediate pain is severe. Far more important is the prognosis for restoring health and alleviating the suffering* (p. 40).

However, it is the couple that must decide what they are willing to put up with, and what sacrifices they are willing to make while they 'pray through' or 'work through' their problems. *Moreover, we are not to coerce others into adopting our religious views, but to enable them to achieve a better understanding of Scripture and of their own faith* (Stone 1996, p. 148).

THEOLOGICALLY/BIBLICALLY

We must bear in mind that individuals who seek pastoral care really come for advice; and some persons will not make a decision unless it is sanctioned by the Church or by one of its authority figures. We need the skill to give advice without being judgmental, without encouraging will worship, and without violating a person's inalienable right to decide for him/herself.

Stone (1996) averred pastoral care-giving requires the pastor's use of a theological template in the spiritual assessment of counselees. He is quick to point out, however, that such a template does not mean that the pastor is rigid or inflexible in his conceptual framework but that the template serves to guide the pastor's reflections *about what has happened and is happening to the parishioner* (p. 27).

Spiritual direction obviates the need for a solid theological foundation. Since we largely operate in a spiritual context and an enormous amount of value is placed on theological interpretation it behooves us to have knowledge of how to reflect on issues theologically. Moreover, a faulty understanding of the Scriptures might have been at the root of marital issues in the first place, and may continue to be a contributing factor to the prolonged pain and suffering of divorcees afterwards.

In addition, not to deal with theological questions is to ignore the fact that people generally behave the way they believe and that the behavior in turn may trigger all sorts of emotional and psychosomatic effects. Knowledge of psychotherapy would therefore be extremely helpful. Nevertheless, we need the skill, mental and emotional intelligence to transpose meaning from one culture to another, especially as we seek to relate the biblical data to our present context.

The following is based on the dialogue between Jesus and the crowd (Matt. 19:1-12). It is obviously an embellished account, but embellished in a positive kind of way; it is an assimilated presentation from the theological reflection located in chapter one. Pastoral care-givers may find it useful in enhancing their understanding of the theological issues of divorce and remarriage and in helping others who are grappling with the same. Let us begin with the original question posed to Jesus:

Counselee 1: Is it right for a man to divorce his wife for any and every reason?

Counselor: No! This was not part of God's plan. He intended marriage to be a lifetime commitment. Marriage is a sacred institution and should not be treated lightly.

Counselee 1: Why then did Moses command us to give a certificate of divorce?

Counselor: Moses did not command you to divorce your wives. He permitted it because of the hardness of your heart.

Counselee 1: Hardness of heart? What do you mean by that?

Counselor: Hardness of heart is just another way of describing our waywardness or sinful nature. This fact predisposes us to treat each other unjustly or makes it impossible for some of us to peacefully coexist. Any deliberation on the issues of divorce must bear that in mind – for the protection of the innocent and for the integrity of marriage.

Counselee 1: I believe that Moses was referring to adultery, which I interpret to mean sexual immorality.

Counselee 2: And I believe that the Law specifically allows me to divorce my wife if I find 'no favor' in her because of her 'indecency.' 'Indecency' I believe include other acts of unfaithfulness besides sexual immorality.

Counselor: It is hardly likely that sexual immorality was a ground for divorce during the time of Moses, since the offenders would receive capital punishment. The instructions of the Law speak to 'indecency,' neglect and abandonment being common applications. On the other hand, in the New Testament, we see Jesus permitting divorce on the ground of sexual immorality. It is apparent that by the time Jesus came on the scene the Levitical Law in regard to adultery was not consistently applied, thereby making room for divorce on that basis, especially in cases where there were no witnesses to substantiate the allegation. However, this should not mean that other acts of hard-heartedness or sinfulness which affect the integrity of a marriage should be ignored or denied. Other instances of hardheartedness which are not mentioned in the Bible may very well qualify as legitimate grounds for a divorce.

Counselee 1: What? This man is a heretic. Are you saying a man can divorce his wife for any and every reason?

Jesus: Of course not! Since we are all agreed for instance that adultery is a legitimate ground for a divorce, let us go back to what adultery really represents. The essence of it is betrayal or unfaithfulness, a reneging on one's vows, isn't it? It follows therefore that any act (within reason) that fits our definition, particularly when such an act is persistent or is part of the offender's lifestyle may qualify as a ground for divorce.

Counselee 3: But why are we having this discussion anyway? What about forgiveness?

Counselor: Splendid! Excellent question! Ideally, this is the right thing to do.

Counselee 1: But what if the person persists in violating his/her vows?

Counselor: Truth is, the matter of forgiveness is an obligation that the innocent party has toward the guilty whether he/she seeks forgiveness or not. This is integral to a person's spiritual and emotional wellbeing.

Counselee 4: I am confused.

Counselor: Okay. You're confused because you cannot see any reason why the innocent should continually forgive the guilty. Granted; this is a difficult thing to do but it will be even more difficult for you if you refuse to forgive. Unforgiveness will eat away at your soul like a cancer. It will make you bitter, and so rob you of the peace and joy of life. Furthermore, it affects your relationship with your Creator, for if you do not forgive others of their wrongdoing, God will not forgive you of yours.

Counselee 4: I see, but I still don't get it, that I have to live with an unfaithful or abusive spouse all my life. This sounds like slavery.

Counselor: Who said you had to?

Counselee 4: The Bible. It says that God hates divorce.

Counselor: It is true that God hates divorce. God hates the fact that divorce has become part of our experience, but sometimes it is the most appropriate response to an unpleasant situation. Let us for a moment imagine that an incurable disease has threatened your life. Now, what if your life could be spared by amputating a limb or by cutting off a breast, would you not perform the surgery?

Counselee 4: I think I get the picture.

Counselor: A dysfunctional marriage creates a lot of 'disease' and it is sometimes incurable. As painful as it is, it is sometimes necessary to sacrifice a member of the body in order to preserve the wellbeing of the other member or members of the family. Plus, sometimes the marriage is already dead; if so, you might as well bury it. You need closure in order to move on with your life. And, sometimes you have no choice in the matter, i.e. the guilty party has no further interest in the relationship.

Counselee 5: But the Bible says: *For better or for worse. Until death do us part.*

Counselor: Where in the Bible do you see that?

Counselee 5: I do not know where to find it, but that is the vow that people take.

Counselor: It is not true that any couple pledged to be a martyr. What they really promised was continued faithfulness to each other, and to cease relating to each other as husband and wife only at the point of death.

Counselee 4: The Bible says marriage is a lifetime commitment.

Counselor: That is more like it. God intends for marriage to be a life-long relationship. And this is the essence of the covenant that a man and woman make to each other. The covenant, however, presumes fidelity on the part of both parties. It is a mutual agreement; it takes two persons to make it but only one person to break it. Now, if one of the party breaks the covenant, the other is not under obligation to continue the relationship, is he/she?

Counselee 5: But you just said earlier that we should forgive.

Counselor: Yes, I did say that. But forgiving a person doesn't necessarily mean that you have to continue living with him/her. That's a personal choice for you to make. Nobody else can make it for you. Nonetheless, professional counseling is always in order, and a person should do his/her best to save the marriage; but one has to be wise enough and sensitive enough to the leading of the Holy Spirit to know when to stay in a relationship and when to let go.

Counselee 5: Well, my pastor says: *God is more interested in our holiness than in our happiness.*

Counselor: Yes, indeed God is interested in our holiness, but God is equally interested in our wholeness. Moreover, not to divorce in some cases may be an irresponsible and sinful thing. Continuing in the relationship may facilitate, if not encourage another person's sinful lifestyle, the abuse of God's temple, the death of a family member, the promotion of false pride and pseudo-spirituality. It may also be construed to be a failure to exercise good stewardship; all of which must be factored in the equation of holiness.

Counselee 5: Are you not contradicting Jesus' injunction, *What God has joined together, let not man separate?*

Counselor: Ideally, a married couple should always honor their vows and so obey the injunction to not separate from each other. But we are not living in an ideal world. There are times when extenuating circumstances may warrant a divorce. So the injunction should not be taken to mean absolutely 'no divorce.' Jesus Himself permitted divorce for adultery, did He not? Moses and Paul allowed it for other reasons. It is really up to the affected parties to decide whether they want to remain married or not.

Counselees All: So you mean to say that it is all up to the couple to decide?

Counselor: Not entirely. You see the integrity of marriage is grossly undermined when God's purpose for it is not being realized. Plus, God has demonstrated throughout history to be on the side of the disadvantaged, persons experiencing injustice or those poor in spirit. God is just as interested in the persons of the marriage as He is in the marriage of such persons. If a choice has to be made, though, between the married and the marriage, it is the married that always comes first. And if wedlock were deadlock then God is able to deliver the living from the dead. God is not legalistic. The law was made for man and not man for the law.

Counselee 4: And what about remarriage?

Counselor: What about it? Remarriage was never an issue in Jewish culture. In fact, remarriage was not just presumed to be in order after a divorce; the right of remarriage was explicitly stated on the Certificate of Divorce.

Counselee 3: Well my church teaches that: *Only the innocent party is allowed to remarry.*

Counselor: Now that is interesting. Then how does your church deal with issues that are not so cut and dry? What about a situation where both parties are wrong?

Counselee 3: Well, neither of them is allowed to remarry. I believe that only sexual immorality can break the marriage vow, and the guilty party **should never** be allowed to marry again.

Counselor: Are you saying that the guilty party should pay penance for the rest of his/her life?

Counselee 3: Well, I think marriage is too sacred an institution for people to break their vows and get away with it.

Counselor: Do you regard your relationship with God as sacred?

Counselee 3: Certainly!

Counselor: How many times have you broken your vows to God?

Counselee 4: I still don't think it is proper for someone to be allowed to remarry after a sinful divorce. God hates divorce.

Counselor: I see that you have strong feelings about divorce. God has strong feelings about it too. We agree that God hates divorce but let's look at some of the other things that God hates:

1. *a proud look*
2. *a lying tongue*
3. *hands that shed innocent blood*
4. *an heart that devises wicked imaginations*
5. *a mischief maker*
6. *a false witness or liar*
7. *a sower of discord among brethren*
   (Prov. 6:16-19, KJV).

Does God grant forgiveness for any of these sins? Have you ever acted proudly or told a lie? If God can forgive murder and other sinful behaviours, why would He no forgive a sinful divorce? Do you believe that Jesus' blood cleanses from **all** sin?

Counselee 4: Okay, I see your point.

Counselor: I am not quite finished yet. Look at what James 2:10-11 says: *For whoever keeps the whole law, and yet stumbles at just one point, is guilty of breaking all of it. For he who said, 'Do not commit adultery,' also said, 'Do not murder.' If you do not commit adultery but do commit murder, you have become a lawbreaker.* Assuming that divorce is sinful, it is not the unpardonable sin, is it? Well how is it that a person may get away with murder and not a sinful divorce?

Counselee 3: You are so right. Thank you for clearing up that issue. But what about the pastor who is divorced and is remarried, should he be allowed to pastor a church?

Counselor: Why not?

Counselee 4: The Bible says he should be the husband of one wife.

Counselor: That is correct. But if we take that verse of Scripture literally then many people who are now pastors would have been excluded from ministry on the basis of their marital status. However, the Bible does say a pastor should be the husband of one wife, but that simply means that he should not be a 'womanizer,' or one that practices polygamy. On account of this understanding, many men are permitted to pastor without being married.

Counselee 4: You mean to say that my church has been giving us a 'six for a nine' all this time?

Counselor: Do not look at it that way. Your church leaders are sincere people, though sometimes sincerely wrong. Only God is right all the time. Man is fallible, only God is infallible. That is why you are commanded to study the Scriptures to show yourself approved unto God. Every Christian has that responsibility. It is unfair to yourself, to your leaders and to your organization when you leave all the theological reflection or Bible study to the leaders of the church; if the leaders are wrong, then the whole organization is in trouble.

Counselees All: Thank you for the insights.

Counselor: You are welcome.

The above encapsulates some of the perceptions of many counselees and that of their respective churches, and likely responses, I believe, Jesus would have given them. We now turn our attention to the fact that counseling should be context-specific or that issues should be dealt with contextually.

CONTEXTUALLY
Counselees' context for seeking a divorce or remarriage may vary from the ridiculous to the sublime. This warrants the need for emotional intelligence so that we may not act surprised or in such a way to embarrass clients. Counselors are reminded not to be judgmental or condemning of anyone although they may judge the situation. Making a moral judgment may have its place later; but the initial focus should be on context. This was the approach of Jesus and the Apostle Paul. Their initial focus was on judging the situation or the contexts of individuals (John 4, 8; 1 Cor. 7).

You may find the Scriptures to be a useful resource. *For everything that was written in the past was written to teach us, so that through endurance and the encouragement of the Scriptures we might have hope* (Romans 15:4). There are specific Scriptures that may be applied to certain contexts, for example, sexual immorality, neglect, 'something displeasing,' and desertion (Exodus 21:10-11; Deut. 24:1-4; 1 Cor. 7). Nevertheless, the issues sometimes are not so clear. General biblical principles may be used, however, to deal with those issues that have no precedent in Scripture.

Most of what is compiled as Scripture was written in response to needs that existed in a particular place in time and period of time. But since we live in a changing world we will not necessarily find the same set of circumstances that existed in the past to be present in our post-modern world. And where the same set of circumstances may be evident, as humankind evolve there will always be our own cultural nuances to contend with, new problems to confront and new frontiers to cross. Yet the prophetic Word speaks to all these, not necessarily in the letter of the law, but in the spirit of the law. Also in the many principles that are laid down in Scripture; and we are given liberty to apply these principles to address our current realities. So the power of the Word lies in its existential value.

Humanly speaking, human development and the evolution of science and technology have been based on fundamental principles, not on inflexible or rigid rules. Accordingly, history has shown that the nations who are the most developed in the world are those who refuse to remain in *'the box.'* So it is with every organization and with humanity on the whole.

Pastoral counselors too must refuse to remain in *'the box.'* To do so we have to keep going back to principles. It is the principles of the Word that gives it currency, and it is the Spirit that supplies its life transforming power. We therefore need to tap into the power of timeless principles, by making the Word come alive in the here and now, and by skillfully applying it to counselees' current circumstances. In order to be able to do so we need to be able to reflect on issues theologically. We also need to be in tune with the Spirit and in touch with the realities of our post-modern world, making use of new and relevant information in the fields of psychology and sociology as well. This speaks to our own spiritual preparedness as well as our intellectual and emotional intelligence. It is therefore our solemn obligation to acquaint ourselves with fundamental (spiritual and natural) principles and apply them in the light of our present needs and in light of the realities of our ever changing world.

One of the criticisms that the Church has faced over the years is that it is not in touch with reality. It is indeed a justified one, for some leaders in their approach to the Scriptures are hyper-literalists; they fail to take into consideration the various figures of speech used in the Bible, and some do not know how to interpret and apply the Word so that it is seen as relevant for today. A typical response on controversial issues is: *God says it, I believe it. That settles it:* But what about when there is uncertainty about what God has said or when God has not said 'it' in so many words?

It is true that some Scriptures may have more than one interpretation and that the Bible does not speak explicitly to every minute detail of life; but we do know some things are right and that some things are wrong based upon the general principles found therein. For example, there is nowhere in the Bible where smoking is called a sin. We are warned against other things like gluttony and drunkenness (Pro. 23:21, 29-35; Eph. 5:18) for instance, but not smoking. Nevertheless, we can deduce from the Scriptures which speak to these sinful practices and others that smoking is sinful because of what smoking does to our bodies; for we are told in the Scriptures that our bodies are God's temple and that we should use our bodies to glorify God (1 Cor. 3:16-17; 6:19-20). Since our bodies are God's temple and smoking has the similar effect of gluttony or drunkenness in destroying our bodies, smoking is also a sinful thing to do because in destroying our bodies we do not glorify God.

Most church leaders are agreed, for example, that smoking is sinful although they cannot show where smoking is specifically mentioned in the Bible as a sin. Yet in matters of divorce and remarriage some passionately stick to the letter of the law in not allowing any other reason/s beside those mentioned in the Bible in spite of the adverse effects of human sinfulness to the well-being of those being affected in a bad marriage. Because a particular 'sin' is not mentioned in the Bible as one which qualifies for a divorce, some pastors are not supportive of a divorce, and thus in some cases contribute to their parishioners suffering or death.

We need to be consistent in how we interpret the Scriptures, generally. In order to maintain that constancy, we need to be careful how we transpose meaning from one culture to the next and not allow the Scriptures to lose its existential value. And in matters that are not so clear, we should not allow ourselves to be shackled by the law, but instead constantly resort to the spirit of the law for guidance: *for the letter killeth, but the spirit giveth life* (2 Cor. 3:6 KJV).

Dayringer (1998) encourages the use of Scripture in counseling. He recognizes its wide use by pastoral counselors to comfort, instruct, or diagnose. He sees the Bible as providing a reference, which may be used to make correlation with counselees' insights into their problems. Thus it may be appropriate to give clients selections of Scripture to reflect upon as homework. Dayringer calls this "bibliotherapy," which he believes is different from preaching, telling Bible stories or quoting Scripture.

In order to apply the Scriptures, understanding the social context in which counselees live is very important. For some couples, divorce is a life and death matter. There may be emotional or physical abuse, incest or other such vexing issues involved, which may be construed as a breach of the covenant relationship or is tantamount to unfaithfulness.

Understanding the cultural context of counselees is also important, for culture imparts meaning. What may be considered normal in one culture may be absolutely unforgivable in another. Counselors therefore need an appreciation of counselees' cultural context in order to skillfully and effectively chart the counseling course.

Context is king in any situation. Jesus provides us with an example of how appreciation for one's context can aid the counseling process (John 4). In His conversation with the woman of Samaria, He demonstrated an appreciation for her context before he sought to meet her need. But that was not all; in bringing her context to the fore, He was helping her to face the reality of her situation. That alone was a therapeutic intervention and a crucial step toward healing. In getting the woman to acknowledge and own her problem – in other words, face reality – He could thereafter influence her in a new and positive direction. Judging the situation does not necessarily preclude some form of moral judgment, but if the need arises this should be done with tact and communicated in love.

Quoting Menninger, Dayringer (1998) stated:

> *No analyst should pretend that he takes no moral position ... Actually, evaluation may be close to the heart of the therapeutic process, because therapy has taken place when individual clients discover new evaluations of themselves and their world. Unless these clients have the experiences of being judged and yet found acceptable in the relationship, they may wonder if the acceptance is genuine or just a condoning and condescending one* (p. 37).

There is a place for making moral judgment, as long as it is done in love (Ephesians 4:32).

COMPASSIONATELY
Unfortunately, the only counseling that takes place in some churches is that which is received through 'preaching;' and it is not unusual for some pastors to attempt to meet their congregations' needs by thrashing their constituents from the

pulpit, by demonstrating a 'holier than thou' attitude, or by giving them the arms-length treatment. Some divorcees lament that the only expression of 'concern' they received from their pastors and from some members in their churches was limited to aspersions, gossips, innuendos and slander. Some people would treat them like spiritual lepers, and in some churches certain functions were no longer appropriate for divorcees to perform. They had committed the 'unpardonable sin of divorce.' Instead of demonstrating God's love and compassion, their pastors acted vindictively and punished them for their failure at marriage.

As a result, divorcees in many churches have their wounds go untended and multiplied unnecessarily. In an interview with one pastor, he remarked: *If some people could not find another man, they would not divorce. They should stay in the marriage, no matter what.* Responses such as these are lacking in spiritual and scriptural depth, also in compassion.

Like Jesus, pastoral caregivers should be possessed of spiritual and scriptural depth, and be compassionate and empathetic toward counselees. Moursund and Kenny (2000) cited Roger's accurate empathy, unconditional regard and genuineness as integral to a successful counseling relationship. These views are supported by Dayringer (1998) who stated that *individuals who benefit from a personal relationship are helped by the love present in it* (p. 37).

Counselors should therefore show and model compassion. A model of care for pastoral counseling necessarily involves compassion. It is this compassion that displaces our pride and moves us to gently restore counselees to a state of wellness (Gal. 6:1, 2). In fact, it is a fruit of the Spirit (Gal. 5:22). Believers are told: *Be completely humble and gentle; be patient, bearing with one another in love* (Eph. 4:2).

Moreover, when counselees see compassion modeled before them and demonstrated toward them they will be encouraged to make the necessary adjustments leading to wholeness. Jesus did not condemn the woman of Samaria who was divorced five times and was now living with a man who was not her husband, did He? He established a relationship with her, showed her compassion and offered her a new beginning. Jesus did not condemn the woman taken in adultery either (John 8:1-11). He showed her compassion as well. Jesus treated the woman caught in the act of adultery with compassion and sent her executioners (her unspiritual accusers) packing. The words of Jesus to the Pharisees and to the teachers of the law are relevant to all of us: *He that is without sin among you let him first cast a stone* (John 8:7b KJV*)*.

The ethos of the Christian faith is restoration, not alienation, redemption, not condemnation. God is a gracious God. The character of God as gracious must always inform our understanding of the vexed issues of divorce and remarriage. And if God is gracious, God is also forgiving. We are therefore constrained by the grace of God to be forgiving as well. Forgiveness is an act of compassion. We cannot truly forgive without showing compassion.

Forgiveness is a sign of God's love and faithfulness to us. It is also a sign of our faithfulness and love for each other. Nothing is more therapeutic than to experience the forgiveness of God; and nothing provides more healing than the demonstration of love toward others and the releasing of those who have wronged us through forgiveness. Therefore, if necessary, counselees should be encouraged to seek God's forgiveness and the forgiveness of others. Dayringer believes that *relationship-focused counselors encourage clients to pour out their souls to God (p. 108)*. Counselees should be encouraged toward the forgiveness of self as well.

Christianity does not encourage the condemnation of anyone, including self. Self-condemnation is manifestation of the sin of pride; albeit a false pride under the guise of humility: for it rejects the grace of God in not appropriating God's forgiveness – in not accepting one's own weakness or humanness, and in seeking to atone for one's own sins by turning on one's self or by seeing the need to pay penance.

The process of healing may be speeded up in a loving and caring environment (Moursund and Kenny, 2002). The environment may be that of one's own creation, or that which is created by the therapeutic relationship, or both. So counselees must be shown love; they should be encouraged to embrace the compassion offered by others, and be compassionate to themselves and to others as well. The Apostle Paul mirrored compassion toward others, when, contrary to his own belief in celibacy being the most desirable state, under the present circumstances, he gave leave for single persons: virgins, widows, and divorcees included, to be married (1 Cor. 7:1-9).

PRACTICALLY

Paul's practical, client-centered approach is worthy of emulation. In demonstrating pastoral care, he was able to set aside his own feelings/desires and focused on the needs of his constituents instead.

Paul also expressed the practical nature of pastoral care in the handling of a case in which divorce was inevitable. As long as there is no desire of a spouse to stay in the marriage, one should let the departing party go *for God has called us to live in peace* (1 Cor. 7:15). In giving this advice, the Apostle indicates his recognition of the importance of continued consent to the viability of a marriage and to the *peace* of the marriage: Irreconcilable differences sometimes affect the integrity of marriage and the peace of those in it. In such a case, divorce may be the only way to protect the integrity of the institution of marriage and for the couple to attain peace and wellness. Apart from taking into account the peace and wellness of the parties in a troubled marriage, it is important for pastoral counselors to take into account the effects of declining marriage to the unmarried (which includes divorcees). There is a practical solution for persons who cannot contain themselves. They should get married, *for it is better to marry than to burn* (1 Cor. 7:1-9). And a divorced person who remarries has not sinned (1 Cor. 7:27, 28).

Sometimes pastoral counselors get carried away with their

concern for the image of the church and their reputation as people who '*fi x things*,' yet fail to demonstrate genuine concern for the people in a bad marriage. Moursund and Kenny (2002) are of the view that it is the client's need, not the counselor's, that must be the primary concern; and that counselors should help counselees solve their problem.

Unfortunately, some counselors are lacking in compassion, too legalistic and impractical, and hence contribute to counselees' dysfunction and alienation. While pastoral counselors may not tell counselees what to do, they can certainly help them to explore options; but too often it is the counselors' need to preserve 'the sanctity of marriage' which is considered, and the wellness of the couple ignored.

Scriptures support the view that any help that is proffered through the therapeutic relationship should be practical. It should be relevant and should speak to counselees' need/s. *Suppose a brother or sister is without clothes and daily food. If one of you says to him, 'Go I wish you well; keep warm and well fed,' but does nothing about his physical needs, what good is it?* (James 2:15, 16 NIV).

Pastoral care-giving is necessarily responsive to needs; whatever the needs are, counselors should be able to give an appropriate response. When the woman, who was caught in the act of adultery, was taken to Jesus, He responded to her in the appropriate manner. This woman was under condemnation. Accordingly, she was about to have life taken from her. Her greatest need at the time was compassion, so Jesus protected her from the executioners. He delivered her from condemnation. But it did not stop there. He gave her back her life. How did He do it? He confronted her concerning that which she was known to be doing, which had placed her life in jeopardy, in the first place. He did not ignore or condone it. He said: *Go now and leave your life of sin* (John 8:11 NIV). In addition, although pastoral counselors need to avoid condemnation, we should be caring enough to initiate confrontation. Egan (2002) stated:

[T]here is a place in helping for interventions strong enough to merit the term confrontation. Confrontation...means challenging clients to develop new perspectives and to change both internal and external behaviour even when they show reluctance and resistance to doing so. When counselors confront, they 'make the case' for more effective living (p. 215).

Egan further states that pastoral counselors should help clients own their problem; and that the goals of counseling should be based on meeting counselees' needs. Thus, if the problem is rooted in morality, clients should own that too.

Pastoral care-giving is an expression of love; and one that truly loves is motivated by compassion to save people from themselves and from the wounds that they would inflict upon their environment because of their "illness." *My brothers, if one of you should wander from the truth and someone should bring him back, remember this: Whoever turns a sinner away from his error will save him from death and cover many sins* (James 5:19, 20). But we are also told to speak the truth in love (Eph. 4:15).

Speaking the truth in love is one of the most practical ways pastoral care-givers can help meet counselees' need/s. This means that pastoral care-givers cannot avoid making moral judgments. Adams (1980, p. 85) stated:

Not only are there situations of all sorts in which judging is essential, but the Scriptures specifically command believers to make judgments (cf. John 7:24). The passage (Matthew 7:1-5) only condemns illegitimate judging. Christ assumes that Christians would find it necessary to judge others, and in Matthew 7 was therefore specifically directing them how to do so. The passage in question condemns judging in a hasty manner, without evidence. Judging others before straightening up one's own life is also forbidden. Judging intended to denounce another in order to raise one's own ego is con-

demned. But judgments of moral value in counseling are precisely what the Scriptures everywhere commend. There can be no morally neutral stance in counseling.

Adams goes on to ask some very pointed questions and argues that acceptance of sinful behaviour is to condone sin and that Christian counselors should get involved in counselees' lives.

How can the Christian pastor 'accept' sinful behaviour? He is pledged to give a proper Christian response to such behaviour. How can he fail to offer known biblical solutions to problems? He is pledged to declare and minister God's word. Shall he sit back non-committally watching the client struggle with a problem to which he can only bring his own hopeless, sinful response, when in the closed Bible on his desk he knows lies the answer that God has given to the problem? In short, how can he forget that he is a Christian and attempt to become neutral and disengaged? Such neutrality is impossible (pp. 85, 86).

No therapy is value free (Goldenberg and Goldenberg, 2004, p. 439). Goldenberg and Goldenberg argue that therapists should not pretend as if they are neutral but search out their personal values and be aware of their effects on clients; and that counselors should be careful how they go about proselytizing others. Notwithstanding, the pastoral counselor cannot avoid getting involved in the lives of parishioners, for noninvolvement is a dereliction of our duty to be our brothers' keeper; to refuse to get involved in counselees' lives is to encourage their dysfunctionality.

Dysfunctionality is a product of unwellness – it stems from a lack of integrity – a kind of discord in our system – whether spiritually, psychologically or physically. It is compounded by our ignorance, or our refusal to face reality, or both. Hence the pastoral care-giver needs to be spiritually wise enough and sensitive enough to know when and how to get the client to face reality.

True, some people are so apathetic that they do not know, neither do they care to know that they have a need. Now that is serious, for they are facing double jeopardy. In addition, some people are afraid or too proud to admit that they need help. On the other hand, there are those who know that they have a need but will refuse to seek help if they perceive that they will not be taken seriously, or that their confidence will be breached. Hence waiting for a call or visit to the office may never happen for some people.

However, wherever persons who are in need are, pastoral counselors need to be sensitive of their circumstance and may need to initiate care. This type of caring is illustrated by Jesus in the parables of the lost sheep, the lost coin and the lost son (Luke 15). A good shepherd does not ignore or give up on the lost sheep; he intentionally pursues and looks out for it until he finds it or it returns home. Like the good shepherd, the pastoral counselor needs to be a person of integrity – one who has the professional discipline and the shepherd's heart – to be able to administer genuine care wherever a troubled parishioner might be.

Based on the foregoing, a model for pastoral care regarding divorce and remarriage should seek to answer the following questions:

1. What spiritual laws may be brought to bear on the situation?
2. What natural or human laws may be brought to bear on the situation?
3. What are the principles involved?
4. What is the context or specific circumstance of the individual?
5. In what way/s is the person affected by his/her situation?
6. In what ways are others affected by the situation?
7. What lessons are there to be learned from the situation?
8. What support networks are available for recovery and growth?
9. What is the desired goal of the individual, or what does he/she want to accomplish through counseling?

10. What is the best practical and spiritual solution?
11. How may the best interest of the individual be served without compromising the Scriptures?
12. How may God be glorified in all of this?

In summarizing this model of intervention and care, we are reminded that issues should be dealt with: spiritually, prayerfully, theologically/biblically, contextually, compassionately, professionally and practically. The model is one which requires counselors, in addition to their work in the 'office,' to take the initiative in forming therapeutic alliances. Such an approach sometimes provides the only opportunity - for some persons experiencing dissonance - for the reconciliation of persons who are disconnected from society - for the reconciliation of truth - for the clarification of apparent contradictions and assumptions of the pastoral care-giver and the care-seeker. It is love in action, as against another approach, which requires the potential client to initiate action in visiting the counselor's setting where he/she may get lost in 'officialdom.' Although both approaches are necessary, the former is sometimes more effective because it sends the message that the counselor truly cares and is not just performing a job.

So, like Jesus, pastoral counselors must initiate action and go into the trenches where the real opportunities exist. This approach is not just suited for persons experiencing dysfunction due to divorce or for persons who are experiencing marital difficulties; it has wide-scale applications.

Admittedly, counseling will not solve every problem nor prevent some people from divorcing their spouse. Nevertheless it increases the likelihood of a successful marriage, and the improvement of interpersonal and intra-personal relationships. Through counseling, couples can learn problem-solving skills and attain a greater understanding and clarification of the issues they are facing and so learn to relate to each other and to the rest of society in a better way. The quality of life in the wider society is contingent on the quality of family life.

9

Conclusion of the Whole Matter

"Let us hear the conclusion of the whole matter: Fear God, and keep his commandments: for this is the whole duty of man. For God shall bring every work into judgment, with every secret thing, whether it be good, or whether it be evil" (Eccl. 12:13 – 14 KJV).

The above verses of Scripture are instructive. It is important that while encouraging people to honour and obey God, pastoral counselors leave judgment to God and not violate a person's right to freedom of choice. The role of the counselor is to help people think through problems and help them to make wise choices, not to do the thinking and deciding for them. Everyone must take responsibility for his/her own actions, for everyone is answerable to God, the final Judge and the One to be feared. We know that there are no secrets where God is concerned and that He also judges motives. We also know that since God is the One who instituted marriage, the family ranks high on God's agenda. These are all the more reasons why we should leave judgment to Him.

Marriage is the foremost institution and is honourable. Marriage should not be taken lightly. God designed His creatures for companionship – to experience oneness and increased fulfillment, including child-bearing, within the context of a husband-wife relationship. It is therefore unfortunate that some marriages end in divorce.

Divorce impacts everyone – the immediate family, the extended families, friends and society on the whole. But divorcees are impacted more severely, unnecessarily so sometimes because of the attitude of the Church toward divorce and remarriage. Alas! In the Church, compassion and sensitivity toward divorcees are sadly lacking. Accordingly, some people view divorcees as spiritual lepers to be shunned.

Since divorcees are regarded as spiritual lepers to be shunned or discarded, divorcees' wounds go untended and their pain unnecessarily prolonged. In the meantime, the Church continues to be divided over the issues of divorce and remarriage. Its failure to reflect more profoundly on the issues contributes to divorcees' dysfunction and pain. Right across the denominational divide, divorcees are hurting, the light of a significant section of the Church having been hidden under the bushel of legalism.

Instead of expressing God's love, many in the Church are lost in the cacophony of primitive theology – a theology belonging to scribes and Pharisees. Yet no religion that abandons or shoots its wounded can make a legitimate claim to righteousness, or make a serious claim to be representing God. Whether the divorce was by default or not is beside the point. God is gracious to all of us, so we should also be gracious to one another: *If you, O Lord, kept a record of sins, O Lord, who could stand?* (Psa. 130:3). Unfortunately, many in the Church keep a record of the "sin of divorce." This study on divorce and remarriage in the Christian Church revealed that a significant number of churches polled administer some form of punishment (covertly and overtly), especially if divorcees are remarried. Aspiring leaders or persons already in leadership are the chief ones affected.

Sections of the Church view divorce as the unpardonable sin. According to them, divorcees' ability to walk with God and to work for God is impaired by divorce, especially if divorcees remarry. Yet by treating divorcees thus, the Church has failed to abide by the biblical injunction: *Do not call anything impure that God has made clean* (Acts 10:15; 11:9 NIV).

Divorce is not necessarily sinful; sometimes it is the most appropriate response to a dysfunctional marriage. And if the divorce is sinful, it is only one of the many sins that God hates, and there is forgiveness for that too. A sinful divorce is not recorded anywhere in the Bible as being an unpardonable sin. The Bible says that the blood of Jesus, His (God's) Son, purifies us from **every** sin. *If we confess our sins he is faithful and just to forgive us our sins and purify us from **all unrighteousness*** (1 John 1:7-9 NIV).

Divorce is not necessarily sinful. Jesus permitted divorce on the ground of adultery. However, we need to take into consideration the context in which Jesus spoke, and be careful not to use Jesus' statement to make wide-scale applications. The Scriptures do not endorse divorce for any and every reason, but in both the Old and New Testaments divorce is allowed for reasons besides sexual immorality, namely neglect, something displeasing, and desertion (Ex. 21:10-11; Deut. 24:1-4; 1 Cor. 7). It is possible for other acts of sinfulness to apply.

Human hard-heartedness or sin changes the picture in mankind's ability to attain God's ideal for married couples. We have seen that where sin has been involved in a marriage, God invariably takes the side of the abused or disadvantaged and grants relief. He does so in order to protect the integrity of the marriage relationship and the well-being of the innocent.

Indeed, there are principles and precepts which may inform one's decision regarding divorce, many of which are still being debated in the religious community. Arguably, the people in a dysfunctional marriage are obliged to obey Scripture and make a decision in keeping with their conscience and their interpretation of the will of God. In the final analysis, however, the decision is the couple's to make; the passing of judgment belongs to God.

The decision to divorce cannot be that of any other than the married couple. In denying the human right to exercise their volition in as sacred a matter of human relationship as marriage, such persons would be found guilty of doing violence against the personhood of the couple in a dysfunctional marriage.

Integral to who we are is the inalienable right of freedom of choice. This must be respected. Marriage is not slavery. It is one of the noblest expressions of freedom. Advice and suggestions are always in order, but in the final analysis the decision is that of the couple. The same applies for remarriage. Paul, for example, in spite of his *better judgment*, showed respect for the rights of others for self-determination, in the case of marriage for single persons (virgins, widows and divorcees). Moses approached the issues of divorce and remarriage in a similar way (Deut. 24:1-4). He permitted divorce because of the *hardness of the heart*. Hard heartedness may manifest in many ways besides adultery, the net effect being the undermining of the institution of marriage. The reality is that if there is no escaping a relationship in which hardheartedness abounds, the marriage becomes a life sentence and a sham.

In cases where the institution of marriage is destructive and not constructive, as it was intended to be, the pastoral counselor is forced to help the couple toward facing reality. Upon facing reality, the affected parties are obliged to decide whether they are going to seek to fulfill God's ideal for marriage by getting their act together, divorce and fulfill God's ideal for marriage with someone else, or make a decision to divorce and remain single for the rest of their lives.

Whatever the decision of the couple, the spirit of the law must be of paramount importance in informing that decision, and not necessarily the letter of the law. Jesus said *the law was made for man and not man for the law.* However, pastoral counselors should neither encourage people to view divorce as the easy way out of a troubled marriage nor be guilty of practicing legalism. Either way, they become a part of the problem instead of being part of the solution.

The solution to the complex issues of divorce and remarriage demands a holistic approach – a model of pastoral care that reflects more profoundly theologically and psycho-socially. The model of pastoral care postulated by this writer reflects the notion that man is not only spirit but also mind and body, existing in relationship with God, self and others. As such, every aspect of one's being must be considered in the decision-making process.

The notion that a Christian couple should necessarily put up with everything in a dysfunctional marriage as a mark of Christian piety is not only unkind but irresponsible as well. God's calling to holiness is also God's calling to wholeness. The essence of wholeness is peace – peace with God, peace with self and peace with our fellowmen. Therefore, the vow: *For better or for worse,* although it should be taken seriously, could not mean slave-like loyalty; it could not mean the voluntary surrender of one's personhood, or that a spouse should tolerate any and every form of abuse.

A spouse needs to know when to insist on the maintenance of certain boundaries, when to run from a life-threatening situation and when to let go of a relationship that is already dead. And if divorce has taken place, such persons should not be penalized or viewed as failures or spiritual lepers on account of their experience.

Since it is scriptural principles that should guide us and not the letter of the law, pastoral care-givers are obliged to constantly re-evaluate positions on the issues; and in light of new and relevant information should adjust our thinking and modus operandi accordingly. Care-givers can do so without compromising the Scriptures. The need to be relevant in an ever-changing world is crucial. When we stick to the letter of the law we become irrelevant in a world that is in constant flux and may rightly be accused of legalism.

Although there are specific grounds on which the Bible allows divorce and remarriage, pastoral counselors should be careful not to allow ourselves to become so transfixed on the 'biblical' reasons that we make no allowance for any other; for in the very unfolding of Scripture, the list was expanded in light of current realities. In the interest of justice, consent to the spirit of the law must always overrule where the content of the law is found wanting.

There needs to be a holistic approach to the issues of divorce and remarriage – a model of pastoral care that reflects more profoundly theologically and psychosocially. The model of pastoral care postulated by this writer reflects the notion that man is not only spirit but also mind and body, existing in relationship with God, self and others. We are relational beings. As such, these relationships are active components of the choices we make and are impacted by our choices.

We therefore need to treat with clients' spiritual, emotional or psychological, social and physical well-being; the issues should be dealt with spiritually, theologically/biblically, contextually, compassionately, professionally and practically. On this score, not everyone will agree. Readers are reminded, however, that popular opinion is never always right. Sources themselves may be people of integrity, but they may be blinded by tradition or limited by their own experience. Being out of sync with reality, they may need to adjust their perceptual framework in order to see more clearly.

Message to divorcees
Do not react to ignorance. Be understanding. In time, people will find their way or see the light. There was a time in our history, for instance, when the whole world thought that the earth was flat, until Columbus got lost and proved otherwise. It is possible that you might have lost your way in marriage so others may find it.

CONCLUSION OF THE WHOLE MATTER

The earth is not flat – you will not fall off the edge after a divorce. You may feel lost and get bruised along life's rugged and varied terrain; but the lost can be found, and the wounded can be made whole again. Divorce may be a difficult stage along the journey, but like other challenges divorce may be overcome. It is up to you to experience *the thrill of victory or the agony of defeat.* Promise yourself, that by God's grace you will be an overcomer and that you will experience *the thrill of victory.*

BIBLIOGRAPHY

Adams, Jay E. Marriage Divorce and Remarriage in the Bible. Baker Book House, Grand Rapids. 1980

Balswick, Jack O & Balswick, Judith K. The Family: A Christian Perspective of The Contemporary Home, Second Edition. Baker Books, Grand Rapids, USA. 1999

Barker, Kenneth: General Editor. The NIV Study Bible. Zondervan Publishing House, Grand Rapids. 1985

Brown, Janet; Anderson, Pat & Chevannes, Barry. Report on The Contribution of Caribbean Men to the Family: To the International Development Research Centre, Canada. The Caribbean Child Development Centre, School of Continuing Studies, University of the West Indies, Mona, Jamaica. 1993

Beit-Hallahm, Benjamin & Argyle, Michael. The Psychology of Religious Behaviour, Belief & Experience. Routledge, London and New York. 1997

Bevcar, Dorothy & Bevcar Raphael. Family Therapy: A Systemic Integration. Pearson Education Inc. New York. 2003

Clarke, Edith. My Mother Who Fathered Me. Compton Printing Ltd. London & Aylesbury. 1974

Culbertson, Philip L. Counselling Men. Fortress Press, USA. 1994

Dake, Finnis, J. Dakes Annotated Reference Bible: The New Testament. Dake Bible Sales Inc. Georgia, U.S.A. 1961

Dayringer, Richard. The Heart of Pastoral Counselling: Healing Through Relationship, Revised Edition. The Haworth Pastoral Press, New York 1998

Dobson, James. Solid Answers: America's Foremost Family Counsellor Responds to Tough Questions Facing Today's Family. Tyndale House Publishers, Inc. USA 1997

Egan, Gerard. The Skilled Helper: A Problem- Management and Opportunity-Development Approach to Helping, Seventh Edition. Books/Cole, California, U.S.A. 2002

Gladding, Samuel T. Counselling: A Comprehensive Profession. Pearson Prentice Hall, New Jersey, Ohio, U.S.A. 2004

Goldenburg, Herbert & Goldenberg, Irene. Family Therapy: An Overview, Sixth Edition. Brooks Cole, California, USA. 2004

Hendricks, Howard G. Heaven Help The Home. SP Publications Inc. USA 1990

Kincaid, Ron & Jorie. In-laws: Getting Along with your Other Family. Intervarsity Press, Downers Grove, Ilinois, USA. 1996

Landers, Ann. Wake Up and Smell the Coffee!: Advice, Wisdom, and Uncommon Good Sense. Villiard Books, USA. 1996

Lahey, Benjamin B. Psychology: *An Introduction, Eighth Edition*, McGraw-Hill, New York 2004

Miller, Errol. Men at Risk. Jamaica Publishing House Limited. Kingston. 1991

Moursund, Janet and Kenny, Maureen. The Process of Counselling and Therapy, Fourth Edition. Prentice Hall, New Jersey. 2002

Oates, Wayne. Grief, Transition, and Loss: A Pastor's Practical Guide. Fortress Press, Minneapolis. 1997

Peck, M. Scott. The Road Less Traveled: A New Psychology of Love, Traditional Values and Spiritual Growth. Touchstone, New York 1978

Reed, Bobbie. Merging Families: A Step by Step Guide for Blended Families. Concordia Publishing House, St. Louis, Montana. 1992

Rice, Philip. Human Development: A Lifespan Approach, Fourth Edition. Prentice Hall, New Jersey. 2001

Secunda, Victoria. Women and Their Fathers. Dell Publishing, New York. 1992

Stone, Howard W & Duke, James O. How to Think Theologically. Fortress Press, Minneapolis. 1996

Stone, Howard W. Theological Context for Pastoral Caregiving: Word in Deed. The Haworth Pastoral Press, New York. 1996

Stivers, Robert and others. Christian Ethics: A Case Method Approach. Orbis Books, New York. 1994

Swindoll, Charles. Second Wind: For Those Struggling to Get Up Again. Zondervan Publishing House, Michigan. 1977

Zodhiates, Spiros. What About Divorce? AMG Publishers, Chattanooga. 1984

Papers & Articles

Assemblies of God in Jamaica, [Position Paper] Divorce and Remarriage. Kingston, Jamaica. 1973.

Associated Gospel Assemblies. Constitution With By-

Laws and Procedures, p.19. Kingston. 2003.

Chisholm, Clinton A. Divorce & Remarriage: Second Thoughts. Unpublished Paper. Kingston, Jamaica. March 2003

The Daily Gleaner. Absent Dad May Lead To Teenage Pregnancy – Study. Jamaica. May 20, 2003

The Salvation Army. [Policy Statement] Approved by International Headquarters, February 1983.

The Sunday Gleaner, pp.8h, 9h. (Faller, Mary). Breadwinning Wives and the Men They Marry. Jamaica. March 24, 2002

The Daily Gleaner, p. D2. Divorced Dad Needs Support Too. Jamaica. June 12, 2003

Society of the Church of God in Jamaica. Divorce and Remarriage [Policy Document]. Montego Bay, Jamaica. 2004.

Other Books by the Author

- Caribbean Crime and Violence: Using Jamaica as a Case Study
- Marriage Under Siege
- Positive Vibrations
- Values Vibes: Instructors Manual (One)
- Values Vibes: Workbook (One)
- Spiritual Intelligence: A Christian Perspective

www.ingramcontent.com/pod-product-compliance
Lightning Source LLC
LaVergne TN
LVHW020930090426
835512LV00020B/3305